I want to believe, but . . .

A Navigator for Doubters

by Boyd Wright

Templegate Publishers
Springfield, Illinois

© 2000 Boyd Wright
Published by
Templegate Publishers
302 East Adams Street
Post Office Box 5152
Springfield, Illinois
62705-5152
217-522-3353
www.templegate.com

ISBN 0-87243-248-3

Library of Congress Control Number:
00-131544

For Jean

with all my thanks and all my love

Table of Contents

Introduction 7
What makes us think there could be a God? 13
Do we have any real evidence? 16
But can we believe the Bible? 18
Are we sure that Jesus ever lived? 22
Isn't the Jesus story just a myth? 24
How can Jesus be both human and divine? 27
Did Jesus really perform all those miracles? 30
Isn't the Resurrection just an illusion? 33
So does Jesus prove that God exists? 36
Are there no other proofs of God's existence? 39
Why can't we prove God from nature? 42
Why didn't Jesus just tell us everything straight out? 45
How can we live up to Jesus' ideal of love? 48
If God has everything, why does He want our love? 51
Why do I need salvation? 53
Does God do it all or do we take part in our own salvation? 55
How can those who never heard of Jesus be saved? 57
If Jesus has already forgiven us, why ask for forgiveness? 59
How do we know God didn't just create and then let things take their course? 61
What does God look like? 64
Why do we call God "He"? 66
Does God ever change? 69
Is God really all-powerful and all-good? 71
Why does God allow evil? 73
Why do good people have to suffer? 76
How can evil be good for us? 80
But why so much evil? 82
Why doesn't Jesus protect us from suffering? 84
If God has everything planned, how can we have free will? 87
How do I know I'm not just making God up in my head? 89

Could my need for God just be psychological? 91

How do we know other religions aren't more real than Christianity? 92

Why has God allowed so many divisions among Christians? 94

Didn't the Apostles give us the final word? 97

How can Christian doctrine be true when it keeps changing? 100

Why can't Christians agree whether God's Kingdom is already here? 103

How can we know what Jesus thought of Himself? 107

Why do we need such a difficult doctrine as the Trinity? 110

How can we dare to think of God as a "Person"? 113

If Jesus is still with us, why do we need the Holy Spirit? 115

But why should we pray to the Spirit? 117

Since God knows everything ahead of time, what good does prayer do? 119

How can we know God is listening? 122

Wasn't Jesus wrong when He promised all prayers would be answered? 125

Why do we need to pray to Mary? 128

Isn't it blasphemy to pray to physical icons? 131

What do we mean by God's "grace"? 134

Why do we need such a complicated formula as "atonement"? 138

Original sin? How can God be so unfair? 141

Can we believe in both God and science? 144

Hasn't science already debunked God? 147

But can science ever help us understand God? 150

Isn't our way of looking at God out of date? 152

Are we humans really so special? 156

What about all the great thinkers who have put God down? 158

Haven't later philosophers discredited Christianity? 162

But how about Immanuel Kant? 166

Why do philosophers make such a big deal about God and "being"? 170

What's all this about "existentialism"? 174

How about that weird "process theology"? 178

Is there a "theology of hope"?   181

Why did God bother to create?   184

How can grown-ups believe in angels?   187

Does Jesus love some people more than others?   191

Why does it help to keep the seasons of the church year?   193

Do we have to be sad during Lent?   195

How can wafers and wine be Jesus' body and blood?   197

Is there a "natural law"?   201

Aren't believers afraid of "playing God"?   205

Which is more important, faith or good works?   208

How can I be good if I feel like sinning?   211

To really believe in God, don't I need to feel good
about myself?   214

Isn't it easier to believe if you had a happy childhood?   216

If I have to keep working at my faith, is it really worth it?   219

Am I supposed to help myself or "let go and let God"?   222

How can I possibly give *all* to God?   225

Isn't it wrong to praise God just so we can live forever?   228

How can Christians be so sure of the hereafter?   230

What right have we even to guess about heaven?   232

What if the whole Jesus story is proved to be a fake?   235

I want to believe, but can I ever be sure?   238

Introduction

I want to believe, but . . .

But what? Because I can't. It just doesn't add up, that's why. I really do want to believe in God and Jesus, and I think religion is fine, but what the churches and their experts tell us just can't all be true. It defies logic. It was all right for the old days, but for an enlightened age it just doesn't make sense.

This seems to be the attitude of many educated, thoughtful, basically good, basically God-fearing, basically Christian-oriented people today. Yes, most of them take religion seriously; yes, they believe that somewhere out there there is a God or a Higher Power or a Life Force or Something. Some of them in a trendy search of cross-cultural adventure may have read Lao-tzu, *the Upanishads* or the Egyptian *Book of the Dead.* But how much do they know of the basic Christian scriptures, of the *Didache,* of Clement of Rome or Ignatius of Antioch? They cannot quite come to terms with much of the Christian data and doctrines which have over the years been proposed in vain to their distracted attention. Most of them in our secular age know virtually nothing of Christian history and would be brought up short to hear John Updike, the internationally known novelist and critic, say, "For me there has been no other game in the existential arena than the Christian creed, no other answer to the dread that one's own mortal existence brings with it."

This book aims to set forth, as honestly as possible, some of the roadblocks that impede an understanding of Christianity. And it proposes answers for some of these problems. It is aimed first at those who want to believe but can't. Along the way it also hopes to spark the interest of those who don't care much whether they believe or not but would like to listen to somebody else's ideas. Lastly, the book is directed at those who already believe but sometimes feel at a loss to explain their faith. Maybe they would like extra ammunition to counter the criticisms of their doubting friends or they would like to build a firmer foundation the better to inform or inspire their loved ones.

You won't find the views of any particular denomination propounded here. These thoughts are meant to be just plain Christian. The book aims to stick as closely as possible to what it seems that Jesus Christ was telling us 2,000 years ago. It will do so by trying to consider, carefully and prayerfully, the questions that most would-be believers and most skeptics have asked over the centuries.

First, a word about faith itself. It's possible that nobody since Jesus has ever achieved perfect faith. Mary could have, and perhaps Joseph, but they were so much on the inside that we can hardly count them. Even St. Peter had a hard time, as we can tell by the questions he blurted out, and we know that at the crucifixion his faith proved far from perfect. St. Paul has given us more insight into Jesus' message than anybody else, but his epistles don't reveal the certainty of a fanatic; instead we find the humility of a seeker after truth. In our search we might do well to emulate him.

In the holiest minds there seems almost always to be a restless tension between belief and unbelief. Think of the most devout people you know. Read Thomas Aquinas, Martin Luther, John Wesley, Dietrich Bonhoeffer, Pope John XXIII. In each of them faith triumphantly fought fearsome battles with doubt.

What then within each person tips the scale toward this mystery called faith? It is certainly the primary, and perhaps the most vital, concept in Christian life. Many believers consider it a gift from God. If so, why has God given it to some and not to the rest of us? Calvin, and later the Puritans, believed in predestination, that only the elect are destined to achieve faith and so come to salvation. The theory was that those favored few were marked from birth and nobody else could win through no matter how saintly a life he or she led. How come the elite were privileged and everyone else excluded? Our Puritan forefathers and foremothers who held this hard doctrine could never explain it; they just knew.

Most of us moderns agree divine Providence doesn't work this way. Another belief widely held about faith was that it is a matter of morality. It was declared to be a sin not to believe in God. This theory died a merciful death through its own illogic. If you seek rigorously for truth, if you search the facts and your mind and your conscience to find if God exists, you are trying to find an answer. To find honestly that the answer to this problem is "no" can hardly be more or less sinful than to find that the answer to 2 plus 2 equals 5 is "no."

That brings us to the heart of our quest. Maybe finding whether the existence of God adds up, whether indeed all this God stuff preached from pulpits and found in the Bible adds up, is at bottom not so different from finding what 2 plus 2 adds up to. In either case we have to use our brains. We have to bring reason and logic to bear. We have to make an effort. We can't just dismiss the question out of hand. Above all, we can't just say that because it isn't immediately self-evident, it isn't so.

For most of us the journey to faith is far from easy. The problems of doubt pile up like a mountain range to be scaled. For some lucky folks, of course, the trip really has been easy. They were born to faith, nurtured in fertile soil by heredity and environment. Faith was everywhere. Those who raised them filled the air with it. These lucky people didn't even need to think; alternatives never occurred to them. They came to believe as naturally as they came to breathe.

Others, almost as fortunate, have been awakened to faith by a single, life-changing experience, perhaps a sudden answer to an urgent prayer, a recovery from serious illness, a seemingly miraculous rescue from calamity. Even more dramatically, faith can fall upon us in a dazzling instant of truth – the flash from the sky that blinded Paul on the road to Damascus, the voice of the child in the garden that called Augustine to open the Bible, the exact hour and moment at the evening prayer session when John Wesley knew. What a way to glimpse the glory of God!

A few find faith through fear. If I don't believe, they tell themselves, I will go to hell. Or, faced with the surgeon's knife or the guns of the enemy, they rush to faith at the point of despair. No atheists in foxholes. When your back is to the wall, or when you are staring at disaster, or when you're simply overwhelmed by the stress of life, you make a pact with your Maker. Sometimes it works. The Roman Emperor Constantine agreed to convert if God gave victory to his army; later, crowned with success, he decreed tolerance for those upstart Christians and so changed the world.

Some people are pulled to faith through need. Theirs is a bleaker, more desolate desperation, a last, forlorn hope, a psychological craving for the security only a Higher Power can give. They, too, are rewarded. They yearn so hard to fill the God-shaped blank within each of us that they actually will their wish to come true. Maybe they are inventing God; on the other hand, maybe God was there long before their dreams were born.

Still others travel a more cynical route to faith. They guess at God and go for the gamble. I will believe, they say . . . at least, sort of. So I'll play it safe. I'll try to be good and I'll go to church once a week. Only I won't give away too much of myself. Those who play this game are hedging their bets, but they are headed in the right direction. They are opening themselves to God.

Lastly, some find the way to faith by an arduous path indeed, by studying the evidence, by weighing the pros and cons, by striving to work it all out in their minds. They debate with others, and, most of all, they debate with themselves. Eventually, they have to decide, and the decision can be agony.

I know. I took this last road myself. I wrestled and fought and tried to come to the truth.

Now I am putting down some of the questions I faced. You probably won't agree with all the answers, but at least you have the questions in front of you. Maybe you can come up with better solutions for yourself. I would add only one caveat. Please don't think you are arguing with God. You are not. I truly believe that right now He is standing by, watching you and loving you.

What makes us think there could be a God?

Humans have always believed that out there somewhere, beyond what we can see and know, there is a Something that rules us and shapes our lives, that must have created us, and possibly even loves us. The impulse to worship, to stretch up toward a Being greater than ourselves, seems to be woven into the very fabric of the human condition. Look back at the most ancient cultures that have left even the slightest and most tantalizingly dim traces of their beliefs and you find hints of a thinking that transcends the physical, of a reaching out to the Other. Cave drawings millennia old, shards and scraps from ancient ruins, the oldest writings ever unearthed, all witness to a groping toward some sort of deity. People yearned for food, for comfort, for sex, for progeny, and found that these needs could be met; surely, they felt, in all of nature there must be a way for the deep-seated yearning for God to be fulfilled as well.

Of course, God has gone under all sorts of names. From the dawn of history men and women have bowed to an astonishing variety of gods and goddesses. The Greeks and Romans knew gods who toyed with humans. Different gods exacted human toil to erect the pyramids of Egypt and the giant slabs at Stonehenge. Even relatively advanced societies kowtowed to gods so savage they seemed to be appeased only by human sacrifices. American Indians prayed to gods that served as totems and acted through animals.

Everywhere in antiquity gods hovered just beyond physical reach yet loomed massively real in the minds of mortals. These gods were truly varied, and the surprising fact is that within almost every culture there were so many of them. To be sure, some peoples considered some gods more important than others, but the concept of a single all-powerful God — monotheism — was a long time coming. Eventually it came to flower at the eastern edge of the Mediterranean Sea, in the minds of a particular race, the Jews. They conceived one God so powerful that He obliterated all others, so holy that they could hardly breathe, much less say or write, His name. Of course the Jews believed they had not thought up this idea by themselves but that the knowledge had been given them, had indeed been implanted within them, by God Himself.

Over centuries the Jews compiled a record of their interaction with this wondrous God. Their writings tell of God looking down on them, taking care of them, talking to them, sometimes arguing with them. God scolded them, directed them, made them, they devoutly hoped, better people, made them in fact more like God Himself. Leaders among the ancient Jews interpreted God's views and became prophets. Others, like Abraham and Moses, told of hearing orders directly from God, and they obeyed. All this came to be recorded in that part of the Bible we call the Old Testament, the old and original covenant with God.

Devout Jews believed, and still believe, that there could be no doubt about the reality of God. Had He not acted and reacted with the whole Jewish people through history? Had He not, through their long centuries of tortunous travels, hovered over them every step of the way, into bondage and out, through battles and all sorts of disasters, both natural and sinful? Had He not taken them into new lands, always guiding, and, for the faithful, always holding out new hope?

Before Judaism, for all those aboriginal people scattered in tribes throughout the earth, the multitude of gods to whom they prayed must have seemed real indeed. But the Jews brought not only piety but also logic to bear on the question of the existence of God. If you have a number of gods, there must necessarily be a hierarchy. Logically, all the gods can't be equal. Back behind them and above them, there must be a single power greater than all the others, that must have created them and so created everything else. The Jews were certain they had found this one God.

Do we have any real evidence?

Christians think we have excellent evidence. Right in the midst of this long travail of the Jewish people, in the midst of travels to distant lands, in the midst of being held by the Egyptians and others in captivity, in the midst of wars and pestilence and hardships, something strange happened. It came at a time 2,000 years ago, when the Jewish nation had been conquered once again, and Judea and Galilee and Samaria, the area later known as the Holy Land and more recently as Palestine and Israel, had become a province of the Roman Empire. A young man named Jesus, from Nazareth, began to preach, and He stood on the stage of the world for some three years, possibly only one, and then, with the Jewish and Roman powers acting in concert, He was crucified. His followers believed He rose from the dead and in doing so brought salvation to every human soul.

Our attempts to understand the message of this Jesus, Who became known as the Christ, have taken centuries of prayer, argument, experience, solid scholarship and good, plain guesswork. But the fact is irrefutable that in His brief life, and in the even briefer appearances reported after His death, the force of His extraordinarily dynamic yet tender personality galvanized those who knew Him. These inspired followers, in the face of hardships and fierce persecution, managed in an incredibly short time to found a religion that has gripped the imagination of the world. The central tenets of this faith are that Jesus was sent to us by God as His Son and that by His own suffering He has saved us from sin and promised us everlasting life. Moreover, the faith contends that Jesus, along with God's Holy Spirit, still lives with us today and that He loves each of us with a direct, individual, personal love.

Thus Christians believe that the life, death and Resurrection of Jesus provide the best possible evidence for the existence of God. And they believe this because these momentous doings are all recorded in the New Testament of the Bible.

But can we believe the Bible?

It may sound simplistic, but if we want to determine whether or not the Bible speaks truth, we have to read it. This caution is not as obvious as it sounds. A couple of generations ago the advice would not have been needed. Our ancestors read and reread the Bible — to themselves and out loud, in the family and in public. They savored it, quoted solid chunks by heart and actually used it to live by. We don't. We moderns argue about the Bible, read commentaries on it, hear a few snatches of it at church, listen to preachers who build it up and to scholars who tear it down. Only seldom do we actually read it.

Why? Maybe modern life moves too fast. Maybe TV and the Internet have preempted the need for a book, even the Good Book. Maybe, in the face of ever swifter scientific discoveries, we just don't find the Bible as relevant as our forebears did.

Too bad, because reading the Bible itself, instead of depending on what people tell us, is the best and most common-sense way to get a feel for which portions should be taken literally and which should be read as allegories, metaphors, fables and good old brain-teasers to make us think. You don't have to read the whole Bible; just dip into parts and pretty soon you can catch the flavor of what is "true" and what is meant to be explanation. The first thing to note is that the Bible isn't one book but a whole collection of them. In fact, the Greek word *biblia* means "library." In the Old Testament we find works of history, laws, mythology, fiction (including romances and drama), poetry, aphorisms, even household hints. The grand purpose of all of these books and all these literary devices is to tell – and explain – the great adventure the Jewish people had in living with and getting to know their God.

The New Testament, only a fraction as long, is, of course, very different. Here we meet Jesus, and for Christians this is the heart of the matter. Again, if you really want to discover what is believable, the best thing to do is read. And this is no great job. The whole New Testament is no longer than an average-length novel. Just go ahead and read it. It won't kill you. You could even cheat a little and just scan the last part, Revelation, which admittedly is tough going.

Okay, so you didn't start reading this book just to be told to read something else. Let's not evade the question: Is the New Testament telling us the truth? The first four books, the Gospels of Matthew, Mark, Luke and John, recount the life of Jesus, and right away this causes confusion. These are not contemporary reports and they are not even rigorously historical accounts. They weren't even put on paper until some 40 to 60 years after Jesus' death, and they depended on what somebody who knew Jesus told somebody else who told somebody else and so on. No wonder the four of them differ in all sorts of ways. We moderns shouldn't have any trouble understanding this. Suppose you hear a report of an event on the evening TV news. Next day you read a newspaper with a more complete story, some of which contradicts the first report. A week later you read a newsmagazine, which has had a chance to gather more information and again differs from the first account. Three months later comes a commentary in a scholarly journal, this time propounding a point of view and making things still more different. A year later a whole book gets into print, and the author, with the benefit of hindsight, includes all sorts of nuances that give us still another tale.

So with the Gospel writers. They weren't journalists and they didn't take notes or use tape recorders. Rather, they employed a custom, honorable in antiquity, of not always reporting what somebody said but, instead, interpreting the circumstances and making up words that they think the subject, to make the point, should have said. Moreover, the gospelers didn't set out to write biographies. Each had a particular idea of Jesus' message and they were far more interested in imparting this than in giving us a picture of Jesus' life. For instance, Mark's Gospel, the earliest, written about 70 A.D., emphasized Jesus' power of healing and victory over evil. Mark wrote a basic account, much of which was incorporated by Matthew and Luke 10 to 20 years later. Matthew aimed his Gospel to reach mainly Jewish readers and brought in plenty of Old Testament parallels to do so. Luke directed his story to the gentiles, even penning a sequel, the Acts of the Apostles, to illustrate the spread of Jesus' word throughout the known world. John, writing latest of all, spelled out the pre-existing divinity of the human Jesus. His is a highly spiritual account depicting a more thoughtful Jesus, less victimized by events and more in command of them. Thus each of the four Gospels is not so much a narrative as an interpretive essay.

Most of the rest of New Testament consists of the Epistles of Paul, James, Peter, and John, and these letters are, of course, even more interpretive, providing a treasure trove of background data on the early Christian era. The letters of St. Paul were written earlier than the Gospels and were sent to bolster the fervor of the new churches this great apostle had founded during his long missionary journeys. These epistles fairly throb with the excitement of the times. Read them and you hear again the bugle call to action proclaimed by the Good News of Jesus. You begin to feel just a breath of those powerful winds of faith and love and hope that blew so mightily through the dawning years of Christianity.

But can all this be the truth? Perhaps it was only the result of delusion and hysteria.

Are we sure that Jesus ever lived?

That Jesus did indeed live is an easy question to answer. We have just as good evidence that a human being, Jesus of Nazareth, lived during what we now call the first century as we do for any of his near contemporaries, such as Roman emperors, Egyptian pharaohs, imperial officials, rabbinical teachers and others. To know that the real Jesus existed we not only have the testimony of the Gospels, the Acts of the Apostles and the Epistles; we have a wide variety of quasi-biblical materials written about the same time or slightly later. Some of these even called themselves Gospels and may have come from the same or similar sources as those used by Mark, Matthew, Luke and John. The early church fathers kept sifting through all these accounts, and by the fourth century they had decided which were the most important and most dependable. They ended by picking only four of the Gospels to become part of the canon of the New Testament. Some of those other older writings, however, give us valuable insights into the time of Jesus.

In addition to this mass of non-canonical material, we have two independent mentions of Jesus by the Jewish historian Josephus, who wrote late in the first century. He is a particularly valuable source because he was not a Christian and his views can hardly be biased.

Moreover, Roman historians early in the second century recorded the doings of that new, hardy sect of Christians. Suetonius reported that the Emperor Clau-

22

dius, who reigned from 41 to 54 A.D., "expelled from Rome the Jews, who had been, at the instigation of Chrestus, a permanent cause of disorder" with their "mischievous superstition." Pliny the Younger as a governor in Asia Minor wrote about 111 A.D. to his boss, the Emperor Trajan, complaining about these upstarts who ignored the Imperial temples and sang "hymns to Christ as to a god." Tacitus, the most eminent of the early Roman historians, spoke of that "pernicious sect" and even specified that the founder, "Christus," had been "condemned to death by the procurator Pontius Pilate in the reign of Tiberius."

All in all, we have plenty of historical documentation that the man we know as Jesus of Nazareth walked the earth at the particular time and in the particular places reported in the Bible. If we are not prepared to believe in His existence, we had better not believe in Julius Caesar or Cleopatra either.

Isn't the Jesus story just a myth?

To be sure, antiquity is filled with legends of gods who die and rise again. The rhythm of nature herself seems to demand some such story. We live the cycle of the seasons, with green things withering in the heat of summer, then dying from the frosts of fall, lying dead all through the winter and finally erupting into new life with spring. All this stirs the dreams that spark the legends of resurrection. But I think there are at least three sound reasons not to dismiss the Gospels of Jesus as just another myth.

First, and paradoxically, the very differences among the Gospels argue for authenticity. These four accounts chosen for the canon of the New Testament arise from separate sources and yet manage to spell out basically the same tale. Sure, each author must have gotten many of the facts wrong, but that's what we might expect given the time span, the difficulties of reporting and translating and the desire of each gospeler to get across his own ideas. The remarkable fact is that the similarities far outweigh the differences.

Secondly, it is the outcome of this story that makes it so hard to swallow as myth. The sheer facts of history keep getting in the way. The followers of Jesus went on to spread Christianity. They didn't disperse and go into permanent hiding after the crucifixion. Quite the contrary. They overcame their fears, banded together in the Upper Room at Pentecost and eventually showed themselves to be gloriously brave messengers of Christ, carrying the Cross to distant lands and with few exceptions almost certainly suffering torture and death as martyrs. Even the bravest of men don't act that way without good reason. Something happened to inflame these apostles. It is that something that demands us to look at the story of Jesus as real.

Finally, the Gospels just don't sound like myths. No one can read them and come away with that sense of the poetic, once-upon-a-time, almost dreamlike quality we associate with the myths of old. In myths we hear time-honored repetitions, the seamless flow of fables told over and over, the cadences of legend and lore. Myths seldom pause to dwell on the petty details of life, the frivolous and the frustrating. The Gospels do. These accounts may be 2,000 years old, but they fairly shout with the here and now. We are confronted with four detailed, thoroughly solid pictures, homely and full of the warts of reality. We glimpse vivid snapshots of the squalor and the hope of village and rural life; we read tight, crisp tales of real people striving to scratch a real living; we feel the pain and the love that bind human relationships. We hear stories we know to be all too human: a wedding where wine runs out; sisters squabbling over household duties; disciples disputing over who goes first.

For all their differences, the four Gospels, as well as Acts and the Epistles, paint a single picture. It is focused and stark and it etches an indelible, unforgettable portrait. It is the portrait of a single, unique man, who stands so tall that he commands the stage in a way no other figure ever has. He lives and breathes and seizes our imagination. He is overwhelming. He seems almost to jump out of the pages right into our minds and hearts. We see this man walk and talk and pray and love. We watch as he bends down to listen with infinite attention and care to those who come to him for help. We hear the wise, gentle, comforting words he gives to a whole range of humanity's problems. The magnanimity, the kindness, the goodness shine through. This has to be someone real. No word portrait ever painted comes close to matching this. The bright light of reality sweeps the very idea of a mere myth off into the shadows. The man who steps from these pages is real.

How can Jesus be both human and divine?

All right, the Gospels give us a pretty clear picture of Jesus as a man. But Christian faith goes a long way beyond that. It claims that Jesus was also divine, that He was sent to us by God, that He is God's Son and that He is God Himself.

In the Gospel accounts, Jesus tells us straight out that He is indeed the Son of the Father and that the Father has sent Him to tell us about the Father and show us the way of the Father. But Jesus left it unclear just how much of Himself was truly human and how much divine. And this mystery plagued the infant Christian church for its first few centuries, creating more controversy than any other problem. Great ecumenical councils of bishops and other ecclesiastics met every generation or so to argue and try to work out formulas to guide Christian theology. Nothing disturbed and excited these men (few women were involved) more than the tantalizing question of the dual humanity and divinity of Jesus.

The battle became so bitter that churchmen managed to spend most of the fourth century fighting over the smallest letter in the Greek alphabet, "i." This tiny letter, known as an iota, stood in the middle of the Greek word *homoiousios* but not in the word *homoousios*. The first word meant Jesus was identical in substance to God, the second that He was similar. The matter was debated at council after council while non-Christians in such civilized cities as Antioch and Athens and Rome laughed at the spectacle of these upstart followers of Jesus wrangling over a ridiculously little "i." But Christian believers took the matter with deadly seriousness. Eventually, those who thought Jesus identical to God won the day, and Christians ever since have proclaimed that in their creeds.

Of course, this doesn't answer the question of how Jesus can be both divine and human. This took more thought, more wrangling and more great councils. The best theory then and now came to be that Jesus, in some unimaginable way, completely beyond our understanding, is, at one and the same time, both absolutely and perfectly human and absolutely and perfectly divine.

Theologians, being theologians, have never stopped trying to refine this mystery. In the eleventh century an innovative thinker, St. Anselm of Canterbury, brought logic to bear and even worked it out as a theorem. Humans sin against God, Anselm reasoned, and God is infinite. Hence to sin against God is infinitely sinful. Such a sin requires infinite satisfaction. Humans can't atone for the sin because they are finite. But since it is humans who sin, only a human can earn forgiveness. God resolved the dilemma by sending Jesus to suffer for us, a being both finite and infinite, both human and divine.

The ultimate answer, of course, is that we cannot penetrate the inner being of the man who walked the earth as Jesus of Nazareth. We will never know whether in the privacy of His own head He thought more as a human or more as God. The best we can do is study His short life here on earth and look for clues.

Being only human, we are necessarily poor judges of divinity, but I think we can find at least two occasions when as humans we can feel the particular force of Jesus' humanity shine through. We get a peek at the all-too-human despair of Jesus when He cried from the cross, "My God, my God, why have You forsaken me?" And we get another picture the night before the crucifixion when Jesus prayed in the Garden of Gethsemane. Here divine powers plainly provided no shield. The terror of the terrible torture to come must have struck the human Jesus exactly as it would strike any of us. Alone in the dark, Jesus pleaded, "My Father, if it be possible, let this cup pass from me." It seems almost as if, in the anguish of His totally human emotions, Jesus forgot Himself enough to ask for the impossible. Then, a moment later, He remembered and so added, "Not my will but Yours." Just for an instant a door opens for us. We catch a glimpse of the perfect humanity of God talking to the perfect omnipotence of God – of God, if you will, talking to Himself.

But beyond these two scenes we have little to go on. The churchmen at those great councils long ago probably got it about as right as we ever will. They knew God was perfect; if He sent His Son to live among us humans, the Son must be perfect, too – perfect Man and perfect God.

Did Jesus really perform all those miracles?

So Jesus, in addition to being perfect God, was perfect Man and did all the man things like being born, growing up, getting into trouble and dying. But while he was doing these mundane, man-like things, He was at the same time performing miracles. How can that be?

The Gospels are very clear about this. They tell us Jesus produced all sorts of events we can only describe as miraculous. As we in our scientific era would put it, Jesus suspended the laws of nature. And He did it, according to the Bible accounts, time and time again. He healed the sick; He walked on water; He made loaves and fishes multiply; He even raised from the grave His friend Lazarus, who had been dead for days. Are we really supposed to believe all this?

To get a perspective we have to project ourselves back into the time of Jesus. It was an age of miracles, a time when science, and even logic, were so lightly regarded and so loosely applied that folk took for granted all manner of things that we today have learned to explain differently. It was so among all peoples, in all customs and in all religions. Signs and portents were everywhere. Look up at the sun, the moon, the whole sky, and you could read riddles. Too much rain or too little meant the powers that be were angry. If you took sick, you must have an evil spirit living in you. Anybody to whom any mystery was attached was credited with an ability to perform miracles. So the apostles and other early followers of Jesus and later the Gospel writers had good reason to believe Jesus to be a miracle worker. It was their natural way of looking at things.

Moreover, the Jews of Jesus' time were expecting someone specific. Their prophets and ancient writers had told them a leader would arise in their midst, a Messiah who would free them from political bondage and guide them to great deeds. Jesus always denied He was any kind of political leader, but the force of His personality convinced His followers that He was indeed the long-promised Messiah. Once they believed that, it was but a step to believe that Jesus performed exactly the kind of miraculous deeds one would expect from a Messiah.

So does this mean we should dismiss Jesus' miracles?

No. The central miracle of Jesus is the Incarnation, the extraordinary, unfathomable fact that God created Jesus as a human being and sent Him to live with us as His Son, as a real part of Himself. This is true miracle, and I don't think there could ever be a greater one.

Now, whether Jesus actually performed all the other, lesser miracles, or suspensions of natural law, as recounted in the New Testament, is beyond our ken. We don't know and we probably never will. From an era of science we can't look back through the mists of time to an era of the miraculous and make a judgment about what then was "real." Yet at the very least these miracle tales can be studied and taken to heart as statements that point to greater truths. For instance, I think some of the stories of Jesus' cures have the ring of credibility. Surely that lovingly forceful personality, that compassionate, insightful nature must have made those patients who believed in Him feel better physically as well as spiritually. Moreover, Jesus didn't heal just for the sake of healing; He turned his art of healing into a lesson of faith. Over and over, He emphasized to the sufferers who came to Him that they became cured for one reason alone: They believed in Him and the Father.

The real point is that whether these particular secondary miracles are true or not vanishes into insignificance when held up to the overpowering, transcending light of the miracle of the Incarnation. What is important is that God sent us the message of His love through His Son, Jesus, and this is the miracle that counts.

Isn't the Resurrection just an illusion?

Since the first Easter Sunday morning scoffers have been trying to debunk the story of Jesus in general and the story of His miraculous Resurrection in particular. The easiest way is to blame the Apostles for making it all up. They were Jesus' faithful followers. They had thrown over their jobs, given up their homes and loved ones, devoted their very lives first to walk the dusty roads of Galilee, then to court the dangers of Jerusalem. Now Jesus had been crucified. The Apostles were defeated and they were scared. What to do? Perhaps, rather than admit their Master was only human after all, they concocted the whole story of the empty tomb. Maybe they managed to spirit the body away, spread the rumor of the Resurrection and start Christianity as a gigantic hoax.

Or maybe those Apostles weren't really dishonest, just gullible. Maybe Jesus had brainwashed them, toyed with their minds in some hypnotic way so that they would later imagine His after-death appearances. After all, we have plenty of modern examples of charismatic leaders asserting their will to manipulate the credulous into a cult. At the very least, those first disciples, disheartened and disbanded after that terrible day on Golgotha, could have been suffering from a bad case of collective wishful thinking. They could have wanted to see the risen Jesus so desperately that they actually believed they did.

The trouble with all these theories is that they fly smack against the known facts of history. Even if this tiny, scattered band of eleven men had somehow managed to evade the guards placed at the tomb by Pontius Pilate, the Roman governor, it would have been difficult for the disciples to get the body away and even harder to convince the world that Jesus had actually been resurrected. As for illusion and wishful thinking, we are faced again with the plain fact that the Apostles simply didn't act that way. They set forth, with extraordinary bravery – and sanity — to spread their faith, and they gave their lives for it. They preached and taught and carried the Good News so effectively that it spread around the world. You can't get that far on wishful thinking.

Then how are we to explain the Resurrection? The facts of Jesus being born in a human womb, of His teaching, of His being condemned falsely and dying on the cross, of His body being laid in the tomb – all these are part of the essential story. They are reasonably clear-cut events, relatively understandable to our mortal minds. Then the tale takes an abrupt turn and becomes even more mysterious, even more difficult to grasp by human standards. The Gospels report Jesus' Resurrection and give us a host of reactions to it. St. Paul tells us Jesus appeared to 500 people. What is remarkable is how varied these happenings are. Paul's own account of seeing the resurrected Jesus in a vision on the road to Damascus could hardly be more different than the experience, say, of Thomas physically placing his hand into Jesus' wounds. Many more people may have believed they had felt the presence of the risen Jesus, and they may have felt this in many different ways. Since then countless Christians have also found their own ways to experience their Lord.

We have to remember that the miracle of the Resurrection, no matter how astounding and how sublime, is like Jesus' other lesser miracles. It still depends on, and is subordinate to, the even greater miracle of the Incarnation itself. God is reaching us through the whole mystery of Christ's life and death and rising again. But with the Resurrection God is sending us a particular message, one that is basic, is absolutely crucial and an overwhelming reason for joy. What God is revealing is that Jesus indeed is still alive for us right now, right this minute, and that each of us can experience Him.

So does Jesus prove that God exists?

No matter how sure you are of God, proving Him is another matter. As Frederick Buechner has observed, "It is as impossible for man to demonstrate the existence of God as it would be for even Sherlock Holmes to demonstrate the existence of Arthur Conan Doyle" (*Wishful Thinking: A Theological ABC*, Harper/Collins).

Christians find their staunchest belief that God is real through personal experience with Jesus Christ. But, of course, this is not proof one can offer to unbelievers. It is not something you can put into a test tube or solve with a mathematical formula. It's the kind of proof that, if you can prove it at all, you can only prove to yourself. This satisfies many believers, yet there are many others who seek more positive evidence.

One of these was St. Anselm, the same theologian who tried to bring logic to bear on the great mystery of the Incarnation. Anselm was studious, brilliant and so devout that he constantly interrupted himself in the midst of his scholarly works to talk to God. He spent happy years as a monk in Normandy but after the Norman Conquest reluctantly agreed to cross the channel and become archbishop of Canterbury and primate of England. While still toiling in his cell, Anselm decided he could puzzle out a proof for the existence of God right inside his own head without observing any outside data. How?

First, said Anselm, use your mind to think about God. Think of Him as the greatest object that can be conceived. Be sure in your mind that no greater object could ever be thought of. But now, said Anselm, if you try to understand God as an idea in your mind, the understanding at once creates the idea of an even greater being, one existing not only in your understanding but outside your mind in reality.

Now you have an idea both of a being inside your mind and of a being out in the world outside your mind. Of these two, the one that is greater both inside and outside your head necessarily is greater than the one that is greater only inside your head. That is God.

Put it another way: Hold that idea in your mind of a perfect being. Now if the object of this idea doesn't really exist, then there is a lack of one element of perfection – namely existence. But God, if the term means anything at all, is perfect. Therefore, reasoned Anselm, God exists.

Put it still another way: Try as you may, said Anselm, you can't really conceive of God not existing. God is that which cannot be conceived not to exist. God not existing is a contradiction, an impossibility. If you conceive of a being who exists only in your imagination, you are not conceiving God.

Philosophers have disputed Anselm's reasoning ever since. Even in his own time, a fellow monk named Gaunilo scoffed. He pointed out that you could make the same argument for any higher thing. You could prove, for instance, that a perfect island existed because an island outside your mind would be more perfect than the mere idea of one. Anselm was not disturbed. His argument didn't depend on what was the greatest among

37

one class of objects. It rested on what was the greatest absolutely. We are talking not of islands, he reminded Gaunilo, but of God.

Ontology is the study of being, so Anselm's theory became known as the ontological proof for the existence of God. But is it really a proof or does it hide a logical fallacy? Seven centuries later, Emmanuel Kant, Germany's formidable philosopher known as the Thunderer, thundered a mighty denunciation against Anselm. Just to hold the concept of an object in the mind does not prove it exists, Kant proclaimed. Then he became even more blunt: You can say a hundred coins in the imagination is the same as a hundred coins in the pocket, but you can't say it's as useful.

Anselm had tried, but even believers have doubted whether he worked out a real proof. Maybe other philosophers could do better.

Are there no other proofs of God's existence?

Great thinkers down the ages have tried to probe the mystery of whether God exists. Many besides Anselm have sought to figure it out not by observing the outside world but by thinking it through inside their own heads. Nobody tried harder than Descartes, surely one of the seventeenth century's most eclectic dabblers. He spent his early years as a man about town and even adventured as a volunteer gentleman soldier. Then he settled down and managed to become both an energetic theorist and a practical experimenter. He probed into mathematics, physics, medicine, but he wasn't content to stop there. He wanted to invent a science that would unite all branches of human thought and do nothing less than explain everything. Like Anselm, he started by looking within his own mind.

If I doubt everything, reasoned Descartes, if I even doubt the existence of a world outside my mind, then I must exist to do the doubting. *"Cogito, ergo sum"* ("I think, therefore I am."). Now Descartes took a step further, a long step often overlooked by non-believers. Can I be positive, he asked, that the world outside my mind exists? Perhaps it is but a fantasy, some giant, complicated hoax. But no, that cannot be. Why? Because of God. God cannot be a deceiver, since then He would not be God. God can only be just and good. It is inconceivable that a good and just God would deceive me. So then I can be sure of this world that I feel with my senses.

39

Then Descartes took still another long step. I can be sure, he told himself, that there is a God for the simple reason that this great idea of a God cannot spring from my mind alone. It can only have been put there by a perfect being. And that being has to be God.

Descartes' near contemporary, Blaise Pascal, thought that he, too, could through strenuous mental effort find his way to God. There was no doubt of his genius. Before he was 17 he had written a work on conic sections treating the subject with a method used by modern mathematicians and at 18 he had invented a calculating machine. His mind darted in all directions, stabbing at one problem after another. His writings were known throughout Europe before his premature death at the age of 39. He, too, wanted an overarching philosophy to explain the universe. He found that his first and biggest question was whether or not to believe in God.

A human being, said Pascal, must make a choice about believing. You can't sit on the fence forever. He weighed the pros and cons and made his decision. "There is more certainty in religion," he determined, "than that we shall live to see tomorrow." With that he resolved to risk all on God.

Pascal reasoned that not to choose is itself a choice. And it is better to choose God because the gain is infinite – nothing less than eternal happiness. You lose nothing by belief and you gain everything. "If you gain, you gain all; if you lose, you lose nothing."

The theory has become known as "Pascal's Wager," and it has delighted cynics for three hundred years. But

Pascal was serious. He was a devout man, and he ended by finding God not only in his head but in his heart.

Thus philosophers down the centuries have shown us that trying to prove God by brainpower alone is a tough job. Surely there must be a better way. Other thinkers have determined to look outside their own minds. Maybe God is out there. Maybe we can find Him by looking around. Could He be, after all, right there in nature?

Why can't we prove God from nature?

Nature herself seems to some, if not to prove the existence of God, at least to point in that direction. Look at the vast variety, the huge complexity of the natural world. It must add up to more than a mad jumble of atoms. Surely only God could have fashioned it. Look at the beauty of a flower, the symmetry of a snowflake, the immensity of space, the grandeur of a sunset, the devotion of your dog. Look indeed at that incredible labyrinth, the mind of a human. The very vibrancy of life bursting all about us seems to demand the presence of a Creator. The world seems almost to pulsate with praise for a Maker.

Thomas Aquinas, the venerated Angelic Doctor of the Church of the thirteenth century, did about as much as anybody ever has to marry theology to philosophy. In doing so, he did indeed look outside his own head and look up to nature to try to understand the world and, above all, understand God. He reached way back into the past and he searched far out into the cosmos to come up with a set of theories that have come to be known as the cosmological proofs for the existence of God. These have fared better than Anselm's ideas, but many have also tried to debunk them. Thomas listed five separate proofs, but they are basically a single argument:

One: Everything that moves must have been moved by something else. Something must have been the first mover. That is God.

42

Two: Every effect must have a cause. Nothing happens unless something else makes it happen. Go back far enough and you find the first cause. That is God.

Three: Everything in the universe is contingent. That means it is not necessarily what it is; it could have been something else. But back of the whole series of contingent things, there must have been something that isn't contingent but instead is necessary. That ultimate necessity is God.

Four: For everything in nature, including human beings, there is a purpose. But when we discover that purpose we wonder what that was for and so we seek again and wonder again. We find we are never fulfilled. We find we are driven to seek a final purpose, and that can only be God.

Five: In our experience we learn to recognize degrees of such qualities as truth, goodness, beauty. Some things or ideas are more true or better or more beautiful than others. But if there are degrees approaching perfection, there must be something absolutely perfect by which we can judge. That has to be God.

Many people believed, and still believe, that Aquinas' arguments go a long way toward proving that there is indeed a God. Others have presented Thomas' ideas in different ways: Somebody had to push the first domino. Or, the universe is like a watch, and so there must be a Watchmaker. Or, who touched off the Big Bang?

Why then do most Christians feel vaguely uneasy about all these efforts to prove God either through logic or by the evidence of our senses? Could it be because we are just that — Christian? Perhaps in our hearts we be-

43

lieve that no proof human ingenuity can come up with is as good as the simple evidence that God exists because Christ Jesus told us so.

But if we are still searching for the kind of proof we find in a laboratory test or in a mathematical Q. E. D., we are apt to find even the words of Jesus puzzling.

Why didn't Jesus just tell us everything straight out?

The process God used, and uses, to let us know about Himself may seem a strange one. God doesn't just lay it all on the line, offer us a systematic explanation of Who He is, hand us a guidebook for Christian theology. Instead, He seems to dole the information out bit by bit, in tantalizingly small amounts, never quite satisfying us and certainly never offering us definite proof.

This, however, is God's way, and it is called Revelation.

Why doesn't God just come clean once and for all, show us everything, make it all crystal clear, banish every doubt? One answer we frequently hear from devout people is: The Lord knows best. He has His reasons.

But perhaps there is a deeper truth. First of all, God actually did tell us a good bit about Himself through His acting and reacting with the Jewish people and letting it all be recorded in the Old Testament. Then God went a step further — a very big step — by sending us Jesus Christ to live among us, to teach us and to die for us. Jesus told us many things: that He was God's Son, that He came to forgive our sins and grant us salvation and everlasting life, that He will be with us always, and that God's Holy Spirit will guide us.

Yet Jesus, despite His miracles, despite His promises, despite His rising from the tomb, never did hand us absolute, concrete, incontrovertible proof. He meant us to believe on the basis of something else altogether. Nowhere in the New Testament is this clearer than in John 20:28-29. The Apostle Thomas has doubted the Resurrection and only been assured by putting his finger into Jesus' wounds. "My Lord and My God!" Thomas gasps. But this is not what Jesus wants. He asks Thomas: "Have you believed because you have seen me? Blessed are those who have not seen and yet believe."

Here is the paradox and the challenge of faith. We are not supposed to see and so believe. We are not supposed to be handed proof and then believe. We are supposed, exactly as Jesus tells us, not to see and then still to believe.

A pretty tall order. Yet this is what belief and faith and love are all about. If we were always sure, we wouldn't need faith. So God gives us Revelation in a very different way. Throughout the Old Testament and the New, He gives us glimpses through a window, hints, ideas to think about. God, it seems, doesn't want to hand us everything on a platter, to make everything instantly knowable. He wants us to come to Him by a different path — the path of praying, of getting to know Him through experience, of feeling Him in our hearts, of learning to love Him. If the veil could be lifted, if all could be known in a flash, if there were some easy, demonstrable proof, then we would know for sure and, of course, there could be no such thing as belief and faith. Moreover, there would be no such thing as meaningful trust in God. More important still, there would be no such thing as meaningful love for God.

It isn't that God wants us to be confused; it's that He wants us to work at seeking the truth. The Bible and God's whole process of Revelation are something far better than proof. They are tools God has given us so that each of us can work our way to get to know Him, so that we can love Him and so that we can feel His love.

How can we live up to Jesus' ideal of love?

Sophisticated people like to point out the different kinds of love that exist in the world. They make a distinction between at least four different kinds: affection, such as the love of parents for children; friendship, such as the love between peers who have common interests; romantic love, such as carnal love and being in love; and charity, the love that produces kindness and giving.

These classic kinds of love seem so varied that our one little four-letter word can hardly encompass them all. The confusion makes it easy to fall into semantic traps. Perhaps the English language needs better terms, something like the Greek *philia* or *eros* or *agape*. We find our little overworked word, "love," frequently in the New Testament, and scholars and linguists have long debated its shades of meaning. But what if, when Jesus used the word, He didn't mean it to be complicated? What if "love" turns out to be the most important word in any language? What, in fact, if love turns out to be the engine that drives the universe?

This is where we should stop to study our own feelings. Sure, each of us may be a bit short on charitable love; it isn't easy to give. We may have trouble with friendships, and in the hurly-burly of life we may even find it hard to maintain the proper degree of affection all the time. Some other kinds of love come easily. If we are in love, we certainly love and want to be loved very hard indeed. And we almost never really stop loving our very closest loved ones. Most of all, we have to admit we never stop loving ourselves, sometimes too much.

Love can take many twists and turns, and it isn't always easy to see how it works in others. Psychiatrist Willard Gaylin tells the story of a man on his deathbed who for ninety years pretended courtesy and kindness while in reality hiding feelings of malice and evil. "All his life," says Gaylin, "he had been fooling the world into believing he was a good man. This 'evil' man will, I predict, be welcomed into the Kingdom of Heaven" (*The New York Times*, Oct. 7, 1977).

Jesus commanded us to love one another, but He did much more: He showed us, hands on, how to do it. First, he showed us that He truly loved the very hardest people to love. He actually sought them out and loved them, much to the dismay of more respectable folk. Jesus really loved the beggars and the lepers and the prostitutes and the tax collectors. But I think He must have known that this is a hard course for us to follow. Jesus, in His wisdom, knew that in loving, as in everything else, we must learn to walk before we can run. So He showed us — dramatically and once and for all — a love that teaches us how to take the first step toward trying to love all human souls.

When Jesus was crucified, He felt every agony that a human being can feel. While He was hanging on the cross, during the very hours that He knew the tortures of slow death, of thirst, of strangulation, when the nails were tearing the flesh of His wrists and His feet, when He was praying to His Father and when He was dying for us, at the most awful and most wonderful moment in

49

history, He managed to deliver a simple, personal message. He said to Mary, "Woman behold your son," and to the beloved disciple, "Behold your mother."

That was — this is – love.

This is what Jesus was showing us. We must start with the love we already have, the love for our nearest and dearest. Then we can take the next step. We can learn to love those just outside this intimate circle. When we have mastered that, we can go further. We all know or have heard of really good Christians who find that they can love those everybody else finds unlovable. The rest of us can keep trying. And while we are learning to love our fellow humans better, something else is happening. We find we are getting closer to God.

Thus Jesus shows us how to love. And He shows us that God loves us. But why should God love us? God has everything, and surely He doesn't need us. Or does He?

If God has everything, why does He want our love?

Right here we come to the core mystery of Christianity. Of all the questions posed in this book this is the hardest to answer and yet it is the most important. In other monolithic religions, God reigns above all, out there, often more a concept than a person. Not so in Christianity. Because God has revealed Himself through Christ, we know He is personal. Christians believe we humans are made in God's image, so God must be, in kind if not in degree, in some measure like us. Put it the other way: Each of us, in a very small way, must be just a little bit like God. The early Church Fathers wisely found that the best way to describe the God Who is so close to us is to call Him a Person. This means that God, as a Person, acts in a personal, direct, individual way with each of us. And He does it with love. He loves us just the way we are. We are all His children, each with a different name and with a different personality and, sadly, with different sins.

Jesus went out of His way to love the sinful, looked-down-upon folk of His era. Today most of us aren't so different from those poor souls. The human race has rumbled along with the same human nature. The ratio of saints to sinners has probably stayed pretty constant. We don't really honor the Golden Rule much better today than when Jesus first spelled it out for us. We all sin, and over time we have learned new vices. In many ways we, too, can be considered unlovable.

Then why does God love us? The closest we can come to an answer is that in our religion, the particular, special faith that is Christianity, we are made in God's image and so God is a Person. And a Person not only loves but needs to be loved. It sounds contradictory: God, Who has all, needs to be loved. But if God is a Person, then He must be the most perfect Person there is. He must love better than any person ever has. He must, in fact, love perfectly. And perfect love needs love in return. Love that is not returned cannot be perfect love. Love, always and everywhere, even with God, is a two-way street. It has to be requited. The only meaningful love is a love that flows out and flows back. We must know that God does this perfectly. God is perfect love. Both ways.

Why do I need salvation?

Salvation is the act of God saving us. Christians believe God sent Jesus to live among us to do just that. Moreover, they are specific about it. They believe the act of salvation came just at that terrible moment in history when Jesus, completely human and completely God, died for us on the cross. Jesus saved us by forgiving our sins and promising us everlasting life.

Why do we believe this? To be sure, Jesus, in His teachings, made this clear, but He didn't spell out as much detail as we might like. For a more complete view we can turn to the apostle Paul.

If we believe in the overriding miracle of the Incarnation, if we believe God is telling us something through the life and death of Jesus, then I think we must believe that St. Paul was divinely inspired to interpret Christ's message for us. Paul started out as a persecutor of Christians but saw a vision and became converted. Christians believe that in that blinding moment on the road to Damascus, Paul really saw Jesus, really received a mandate not only to spread the Good News but also to explain it.

The core of what Paul tells us is that we all sin all the time, but God loves us so much that He has already forgiven us. God sent Jesus to be with us and to show us this forgiveness. Now, since this has happened, our aim in life should be to be so thankful for this great undeserved gift of forgiveness and to love God and Jesus with such joyful gratitude, that we really do become good and really act as God wants us to.

This does not mean that we are perfect or ever will be. But it does mean that because of our grateful faith, because our hearts are so filled with true thanks and love, we will do what God wants us to do most of all. That is, we will turn to Him of our own free will, lovingly, happily, openly. Through our genuine acceptance and trust, we will become better persons. We will, in fact, become good enough to receive God's salvation.

It is not a matter of doing good works to earn salvation. This is not the route Paul shows us. Yes, we will end by doing good deeds, but the motive will be far different. We will not perform works in order to achieve salvation; we will do them because we are so thankful, because we love God so much. We will live a moral, godly life, and we will live it freely, gladly, with such a loving, happy heart that we could never think of doing anything else.

Salvation means that we have come to love Jesus with all our hearts, that we love Him so much that there is no room for sinning. We love Him so much that we want to be good.

Does God do it all or do we take part in our own salvation?

There are good Christians who believe humans play no part in their own salvation and that God has done the whole job for us. Logic, in a sense, is on their side. They contend that God has already forgiven our sins as an unmerited, no-strings-attached gift and that we haven't had to lift a finger to achieve this. Thus, the argument goes, we don't need to do anything, indeed cannot do anything, to save ourselves.

I think this view has merit, but I don't think it goes far enough and that it leaves out a vital factor. This is that God, along with this undeserved, absolutely free gift of forgiveness, has given us something else. This other gift is free will. You have it, I have it, everybody has it. God wants us to use this free will because He loves us. He wants each of us, in our own way and in our own time, to turn to Him voluntarily and with love. He wants us to act. When we do this, I believe, we are playing a role in our own salvation.

God sent Jesus to live among us and to forgive our sins. Christians believe that this great forgiveness came when Jesus suffered crucifixion and died for us. Whatever happened in that one, miraculous moment on the cross is far, far beyond our human comprehension. But that moment was so enormous for all humanity and yet so wonderfully personal for each of us that I feel certain we must have played a part in the forgiveness and must still be playing a part.

There are all sorts of ways of picturing what happened on Calvary at that most terrible and most precious moment in all eternity. Maybe the view that God acted alone and we humans were passive is correct. But I don't think so. My heart, all my feelings, tell me otherwise. In my mind the image of our Lord hanging on the cross, suffering and dying for us, is etched with terrifying clarity. Amid the awful agony I can see Him lean down to me. And I can see another picture, too. I can see me trying to reach up to Him.

How can those who never heard of Jesus be saved?

If Jesus came to grant us salvation, what happened to all the millions of people who died before He appeared? Were they denied Jesus' promise of eternal life or even condemned to hell because Jesus wasn't there to forgive their sins? What about the souls living today who by accident of geography or illiteracy or poverty have never had a chance to hear the Good News?

First of all, since we know God's mercy is infinite, we can be sure He finds ways to reach everyone eventually. Certainly He is not being unfair due to a vagary in the celestial calendar. Depend upon it, He loves those born B. C. just as much as those born A. D. Nonetheless, the numbers seem puzzling. Only a handful of folk were able to hear Jesus preach. And only in the last two millennia have any of us been able to read the Gospels. An overwhelming majority of the human race has lived and died without hearing the name Jesus Christ. Why didn't God choose to trumpet His momentous message right from the beginning of humanity?

I think the answer lies in the dual nature of time. Years, weeks, hours are vital to us. We can't plan or even think without them. We're trapped in the web of time. We can measure the exact days we have spent alive and we can compute all too well the span we have left. Time has ruled us from the cradle and will count us tick by tock into the grave.

But all this lies in the realm of earth-bound mortality. Where God lives time has another nature. Perhaps it doesn't exist at all. Certainly God needs to take no note of it. He doesn't care if we lived 10,000 years ago or if we died last week. To Him we are all the same. He can hear all the prayers, pronounce all the blessings and spot all the sins of all of us in a single second. He has pledged that all who truly turn to Him will live with Him in heaven forever. Surely such a stupendous promise must stretch both backward and forward through time. When we reach that home He has prepared for us, we will find no clocks and no calendars on the wall.

So we must believe God can indeed reach everyone. No years and no geography can stand in His way. Through the vastness of time and space He has surmounted all those merely physical barriers that seem so confining to us. We can be sure that His love knows no bounds.

If Jesus has already forgiven us, why ask for forgiveness?

A Christian's prayers are filled with asking for forgiveness. The very prayer that Jesus taught us to say asks God, "Forgive us our trespasses." Yet the bedrock of Christian belief is that Jesus Himself came to us here on earth to live with us and to die on the cross specifically to forgive our sins. If the job was done for us all those years ago, why should we pray now for forgiveness? How is it possible in logic to ask for something we already have?

One answer might be that Christ died to save us from the original sin of all humankind but that each of us has to seek forgiveness for the particular, individual sins we are responsible for.

Another answer might be that Jesus died to give us a chance to earn forgiveness. Under this theory Jesus narrowed the gap between God and ourselves but left the last step up to us. He thus paved the way for each of us to work out our own salvation.

Good answers, but I think I have a better one. I believe that Jesus really did forgive all our sins, big and small, original and individual, and that we are already saved. I believe Jesus, by dying for us on the cross, did the job completely, no strings attached. I believe that through Jesus God has given us an incredibly generous, unearned gift, the gift of His grace. I believe that you and I haven't lifted a finger to deserve this but that we still have been forgiven and that right this minute we can be fully one with God.

But I also believe that now that this has been done, each of us still has a role to play. We have been forgiven, but we are still free to accept or reject that forgiveness. We are free to accept or reject God Himself.

How do we accept God? How do we accept this gift of forgiveness?

By working at those sins. We have been forgiven, but, unfortunately, for most of us those sins are still with us. We have to show God that we are so grateful to Him, that we love Him so much for His generosity that we are truly repentant, that we truly detest our sins and that we really want to do better. Then we have to keep working at the job. We have been given a great unearned gift, to be sure, but the task is not done. We have to do our part. Nobody said being a good Christian is easy. The effort never stops.

So we thank God for His wonderful forgiveness and we implore Him to help us live up to our promises to try to do better. Always, the ultimate goal is to be so grateful and to love God so much that we want truly to be good.

How do we know God didn't just create and then let things take their course?

This question goes to the heart of the difference between theism and deism. Both words stem from root words for god, but each presents a particular kind of god, very different indeed from the other. Most main-line Christians today are theists, but the deists can make a pretty good case for themselves.

Deism is a belief that became popular in the 17th century. It was born in England, perhaps because people wearied of the rigors of Puritanism. It spread to the continent and to the colonies and really blossomed in the 18th century, traveling hand in hand with the age of Enlightenment. Deism places God alongside the world but not in it. It holds that God created the universe, then stepped aside to let things spin along by themselves. The Watchmaker made the watch and wound it up, but that's all. The watch keeps ticking, and God has withdrawn and left human beings to be guided by their own reason. No revelation, no miracles. Not even any Christ except as a great teacher.

Deism was big in its day. In France Voltaire embraced it. In America we can count Franklin, Washington, Jefferson and many other Founding Fathers. They were always talking about the Creator, but they didn't put much stock in the divinity of Jesus.

This notion that God started everything but acts as an absentee Lord finds some popularity today even if its proponents no longer call it deism. Plenty of people be-

61

lieve a Higher Power is back of everything, but they don't think He is the personal God other Christians pray to. They believe that maybe He isn't a he at all but rather some kind of Life Force. They think this Force once breathed life and everything else into existence but now just sits back and lets the good times and the bad roll on.

This is a far cry from the personal, loving God most Christians believe speaks to them and answers their individual prayers. But let's not knock the deists. They were and are devout folk and some of them possessed the greatest minds we've known. I can profit from them. Too often I fall into a trap of putting God into a time frame, of conceiving Him watching over the world and standing ready to intervene whenever He finds it necessary. I think of Him of acting like a busy architect supervising a construction site or a careful captain conning a ship through shoal waters.

The deists, in many ways, had a wiser concept. They believed God could make the world then leave it alone, that His handiwork was so perfect that He managed to will whatever He wanted in a single instant. They believed He could have started all the causes and all the effects there have ever been and ever will be with a single snap of His fingers or a single flash of His infinite creativity. They knew that God has never needed to change anything, ever, that He did it all, once and forever. They knew that God never needs to live within time and that no natural law, even the law of causation, binds God.

Thus the deists serve as a good corrective for those of us who think God is always intervening. God knows best and, of course, we can never know just how much

He, in His infinite wisdom, is acting directly and to what degree He is letting things take their course. But I think the deists miss an essential point. God is indeed personal. We have to know that He is always acting. Right now, this very minute, He is here with each of us. That is the essence of Christianity.

Those of us who believe in a personal God are theists. We believe in the divinity of Jesus. We believe in the God Who loves us so much that He sent His own beloved Son to live with us, to be tortured and killed on the cross for us, to save us from sin and give us everlasting life. As theists, we can feel the presence of this wonderfully intimate God. We feel Him infinitely close to us. We can't always know when God is "intervening" and when He isn't, but we can know that, in a personal, loving way, He is always with us.

What does God look like?

In this flibbertigibbet age, when everybody wants to picture God in his or her own way, it's useful to go back to one of the greatest Christians of all. St. Augustine, writing 1,600 years ago, set down definite rules about how one should — and should not — visualize our Creator.

In an essay entitled "Homilies on 1 John," commenting on a sentence in the epistle, "No man has ever seen God at any time" (4:12), Augustine begins by telling us, "God is an invisible reality: He is to be sought, not with the eye, but with the heart." Then Augustine goes on to list common ways people picture God: "One may easily imagine for oneself some vast form, or some measureless immensity extended through space, as it might be this light which our eyes can see, increased to the limit and flooding the landscape; or one may picture some old man of venerable aspect."

That last image, an "old man of venerable aspect," still sticks as a picture for God with many of us. It's easy to see God as a kindly, elderly gentleman with a long white beard dressed in a flowing robe and bearing a shepherd's crook. But Augustine does not accept any of these models. "Our thoughts are not to go that way," he warns, and he goes back to comment on the First Letter of John. "There is true matter for your thought, if you would see God. 'God is love' (4:16). What outward appearance, what form, what stature, hands or feet, has love? None can say; and yet love has feet, which take us to Church, love has hands which give to the poor . . . He that has charity sees the whole at once . . . My brothers, one does not love what one cannot see."

Augustine's argument is that God is invisible, and we humans can't see Him. Yet God is love, and Augustine, by painting his vivid images, shows that we can easily picture good deeds and so can visualize love. Thus, according to this great theologian of the early church, through love, we can find God, understand Him and see Him.

Today we moderns tend to scoff at the question: What does God look like? It's a question for children, not adults. But to quest for an answer is a good way to keep ourselves humble. Augustine's image of God as love is a guide for living.

And while we're at it, we might remember something else. Too often, when thinking about God, even if we are not trying to imagine Him physically, we fall into a trap and forget about love. If we insist God is personal, we are intolerant of those who imagine Him as a Power or Force. If we imagine God as male, we get annoyed at those who perceive Her as female. We indulge ourselves in feelings that are the very opposite of love.

Augustine provides a way out of this trap of intolerance. He tells us to focus on love. Think of God as love, and if we try hard enough, we may see Him.

One thing is sure. We will never visualize God at all if we don't start by being tolerant of the views of our fellow humans. What does God look like? Maybe we should get on our knees and ask Him.

Why do we call God "He"?

Does God care what we call Him/Her/It?

You bet He/She/It does. How do I know? Because God wants you and me to make a vital decision, whether or not to come to Him/Her/It.

I wish I could have written that without those clumsy personal pronouns. But when we talk about God we have to get personal. To make that big decision whether or not to turn to God we have to think about God, and to do that we have to hold Something in our minds. Your image may be different from mine, but I respect it.

This brings us to the debate over "inclusive language," which has been bedeviling some churches. "Horizontal" inclusive language shouldn't really be much of a problem. It is simply concerned with whether certain terms like "man" or "men" refer to males only or to human beings of both sexes. Until well into the 20th century nobody gave this a thought. The Bible, Shakespeare, Milton and all the old writers used "man" to refer to everybody. Then, because the human race has so often in so many ways been unfair to women, we began to get self-conscious, and some well-meaning souls decided that the use of "man" to refer to both genders was sexist. So now we have learned to be careful and to substitute other words like "people" or "we" when we want to talk about everybody.

No great harm here, it seems to me, as long as we try not to devalue our language too much. If the use of this inclusive language in public prayer moves even one person closer to God, I'm all for it. After all, the job of churches is to help us reach God, not to throw up obstacles.

Efforts have been made to alter the words of prayers and other parts of public worship without destroying the meaning or the power and beauty of the prose. Many of these changes have been successful, and we can expect more. Thus "horizontal" inclusivity is less of an issue now than it was even a short time ago. But "vertical" inclusive language is another matter altogether. This concerns how we speak about God.

Can we talk about God without being sexist? Suppose we apply the same test we used for horizontal language. How can we choose words that will bring each of us closer to God? In some religions worshipers can shape any image of God they want. But the first point to remember is that if we are practicing as Christians, if we gather in a Christian church or elsewhere, we do so because we believe the specific message of Christ. This means we have to build whatever image we make upon what Christ told us. He told us the same thing over and over. He made no bones about it. He called God "Father."

Now there is nothing feminine about a father. He is about as masculine as you can get. To be sure, some good Christians take comfort in thinking of God as a Mother or a Lover or a Friend. If that helps them get closer to God, again I'm in favor of it. But I think they are missing out on something. I think the picture Jesus gives us of God is the clearest, the most accurate and the most helpful of all.

Go back to the Old Testament. In book after book, the ancient tradition tolls like a mighty bell. It rings with one, strong, unforgettable message: the God above us is in every way our Father.

Then comes the New Testament with the greatest theologian of them all. Jesus paints a picture that can never fade. Look up, look within, look everywhere. There you will find Abba, God the Father. Jesus gives us no other image. No blurring, no choices. Just God – the Father.

If we let other concepts cloud this picture, we miss a vital part of Christianity. If we try to include everybody's pet idea, if we try to be too inclusive, we end with a watered-down version of God. For a Christian to live without the Father is a terrible, empty sadness.

In the millennia to come, we may be sure believers will come up with all kinds of creative ideas to visualize God. They will find new ways to journey to Him. But I think the path Jesus has shown us will be the surest of all.

Does God ever change?

Traditional theology holds that God, in addition to being all-wise, all-powerful, all-good and all just about everything else, is also immutable, that is, unchanging. God, this thinking goes, has no need to change and so does not and never has. He has been exactly the same forever in the past and will stay the same forever in the future.

However, some modern theologians, among them Father David Tracy, a Roman Catholic, have questioned this traditional concept. "Is not the God of Jewish and Christian scriptures," Tracy asks, "a God profoundly involved in humanity's struggle to the point where God not merely affects but is affected by the struggle? . . . Can the God of Jesus Christ really be *simply* changeless, omnipotent, omniscient, unaffected by our anguish and achievements?"

Father Tracy puts his finger on a paradox of Christianity. How can God be both unchanging and changing? I think I can just see how. In a sense God is two-fold. In one way, He is out there, immutable, above all, beyond all, immense, embracing, enveloping, enfolding the universe, the total One for everyone everywhere. In this way He never changes.

Yet at the same time God is something different. For each one of us He is infinitely private and personal. When He acts for me, He acts only for me. He is inside me and also just outside me, reaching for me and touching me. Because I don't always act properly, because I sin, God knows the failure of rejection. If I act as I should, God knows the joy of success. Thus, He not only affects me but also is affected by me. Here the changeless One is forever changing because He and I have a real relationship: I react to Him and He reacts to me.

Can I dare to hope that God changed just a little bit when I said my prayers to Him this morning?

Is God really all-powerful and all-good?

How can we mere mortals decide what God is like, figure out what His attributes are? It's tough, but God gave us brains and it's a safe bet He wants us to use them. Instead of throwing up our hands and moaning that we can't possibly begin to know, there are some things we can do. For starters, if we really want to find out what we can about God, we can examine Scripture, learn from the ancients, heed theologians past and present and, above all, use our own powers of logic and of imagination.

Traditional theology says that God, among other things, is omnipotent, that is, all-powerful. Why do we think so? Couldn't God be just a Force contending against evil, perhaps improving the world gradually? If so, then God would not be omnipotent. And if He is not omnipotent, then He must depend on Something Else, some primal force that does control both good and evil. And what could that Something Else be but God? We find we are going in a circle. It seems pretty clear that if we believe in God at all, it makes sense only to believe that He is all-powerful.

Traditional theology also maintains that God is all-good. Do we have any real basis for thinking so? Couldn't God be part good and part evil — a kind of split personality? After all, most things we know seem part good and part evil and even the personalities of most individual people we know seem split this way. Why not God? Couldn't there be, in fact, two Gods, one good and one evil, fighting for possession of the universe? Believers in some well-known religions propound this thesis, among them the Manichees of antiquity and, more recently, the Zoroastrians, who still flourish in India and elsewhere. But this is dualism, not Christianity. For Christians, Christ Himself provides the best denial of the concept of dualism. There is nothing in Jesus' life on earth that remotely suggests a part-good, part-evil God. Jesus Himself was all-good. If we believe in Jesus, it makes sense to believe only in a God Who is all-good.

But if we agree that God is all-good and at the same time all-powerful, this opens up a very big question indeed.

Why does God allow evil?

If God is all-powerful and all-loving, why does He allow evil? Since the dawn of religion this question has bedeviled believers and delighted skeptics. The problem is so famous it has its own name, "theodicy." It strikes to the very heart of the nature of God.

Everywhere in our world we find both good and evil. We see good things but we also see an awful lot of just plain nastiness. Life seems to be one long struggle for survival. The good and the bad run on and on together, and we have learned to take them for granted. But if we have a wise, benevolent God Who can do anything, order anything, why should He permit the bad stuff to exist? Why doesn't He provide a universe where everybody is happy, healthy and well cared for?

Some good Christians answer the question by begging it. They throw up their hands and say, "God knows best" or "The Lord moves in mysterious ways." Sometimes they even declare, somewhat illogically, "God knows what's best for us." Their faith is commendable, but their intellectual and spiritual curiosity could use a shaking up.

If we seek guidance from the Bible for the problem of why God allows evil, we get what might be one answer right at the beginning, in the story of Adam and Eve. The tale tells us a good deal about life, as long as we're careful not to take it literally. It isn't meant to be a scientific explanation for the start of the human race. It's meant to be wisdom, and it is. "Adam," in fact, is the Hebrew word for "man" and "Eve" for "life."

In the story, Adam and Eve, the first human beings, are happy in paradise. God has given them everything they need but has ordered them not to take fruit from the Tree of the Knowledge of Good and Evil. Then the Serpent comes slithering along and tempts Eve to do exactly what she has been told not to do. She succumbs and gives some of the fruit to Adam. When God appears, Adam blames Eve and she tries to blame the whole thing on the Serpent. God is stern. He tosses Adam and Eve out of the Garden of Eden into the cruel world. Here Eve is sentenced to the ordeal of childbirth and both have to put on clothes, work for a living and struggle for survival.

The wise writers of this Creation story in Genesis have made Adam and Eve to stand for Everyman and Everywoman and the Serpent to stand for evil in general and temptation in particular. The writers' purpose is to explain the great mystery of God's relationship to each human being. The story means that every individual person is given a chance to accept or to reject God. God wants each person to come to Him voluntarily, of his or her own free will. We can either turn to God, love Him and be good, as He wants us to be, or we can succumb to temptation, do only the things that please us and live an evil life. Each of us must make this choice. Adam and Eve chose to reject God, and so they were banished from Eden.

Of course we don't live in a Garden of Eden. We live out in that same real, nitty-gritty world that Adam and Eve were sent to. It is here, in the midst of problems all around us, in the midst of scratching for a living, in the midst of treating our fellow human beings either kindly or badly, in the midst of making choices, that we make the Big Choice. This is the decision whether to ignore God and live as our appetites tempt us to live or to accept God and live as He wants us to live.

God wants us to make a real choice. And the choice can't be a real one if we can make it wrapped in a cocoon of paradise where God already has done everything for us. The decision has to be made in a real world where the living isn't always easy. We can turn to God and give Him real love only against a background of real life and real struggle.

This, then, may be a very good reason why God has made a world filled with both good and evil for us to live in. But this answers only part of the question of why God allows evil. There's more.

Why do good people have to suffer?

We are making progress. We have decided that God allows evil to exist, but it is men and women, the followers of Adam and Eve, who make bad choices and so bring the evil upon themselves. But, of course, there is another kind of evil abroad in our world. We can't blame human beings for everything. Not all the evil in the world is man-made. Human death is often not brought about by humans alone. Tornadoes and earthquakes strike from nowhere and kill thousands; disease takes the lives of innocent children.

Every day we hear of sheer, pure evil happening to even the best of people:

♦ A patient suffers the agony of cancer for months before dying. Why, we ask, if God is all-powerful and all-good, doesn't He show mercy and end the life sooner?

♦ A child is born mentally defective and not only leads a seemingly useless life but causes years of grief for loving parents. Why couldn't God have let the child be born whole or at least prevented it from being born at all?

♦ An invalid mother or aunt or grandfather lives for years and destroys the chance for temporal happiness of somebody who devotes her life selflessly to caring for the patient. Is God showing mercy? Or even simple justice?

76

♦   Millions of infants are born into a world where their only fate can be want – in Asia, in Africa, in the ghettoes and poverty belts of our own country. Why does a loving, omnipotent, *good* God allow it?

Now we have reached the heart of the question. Everywhere about us there seems to be hideous evil, and a great deal of it cannot be due to the greed and bungling of human beings.

If we go back again to the Bible to ask why God allows good people to suffer, we find one answer in the Book of Job. Here we meet a prosperous and unusually devout man upon whom God suddenly inflicts terrible and apparently inexplicable disasters. Job's children, his servants, his livestock are all killed. He himself is scourged by sores all over his body. Three friends come to comfort Job and make matters worse by insisting that he must have sinned badly to merit God's punishments. But Job really is good. Finally, driven to despair, he confronts God with the question of why an innocent man must suffer. God reminds Job that he is but a tiny part of creation and yet presumes to judge God. Job is immediately contrite and offers God his complete trust. Some of the calamities are then lifted.

The tale is a dramatic account of one man's faith. Its message is that each of us, no matter what and in spite of everything, must never lose our trust in God. But the story doesn't get to the nub of the question of why humans have to suffer.

Philosophers and theologians have strained to solve the problem. One theory, prevalent in the old days but out of favor with modern folk, is that God sends us ad-

77

versity to purify us. The idea is that if we suffer enough, if we manage to survive enough daunting ordeals, we come out of it all as stronger people. Thus God creates evil to make us better. He uses tough love to shape us on the fiery forge of suffering.

Over time other thinkers have perceived a gentler side of God. Thomas Aquinas, writing in the 13th century, declared that God allows evil to bring out the goodness in the good. "Good is rendered more estimable," he said, "when compared with particular evils. For example, the brilliance of white is brought out more clearly when set off by the dinginess of black. And so, by permitting the existence of evil in the world, the divine goodness is more emphatically asserted in the good."

Five hundred years later, a German philosopher named Gottfried Wilhelm Leibniz had another idea, which would become more famous. It is he who coined the term "theodicy" (from the Greek *theos* for god and *dike* for justice) to mean "justifying God for the evils of the world."

Leibniz was a true eclectic genius. Not only did he discourse on logic and ethics, he dabbled in science and is considered the inventor of calculus. In between he earned a doctor-of-laws degree and held governmental posts in Brunswick and Hanover.

Leibniz's great idea was that if God is a perfect being and creator of the world, He must have chosen to create the best of possible worlds, and we must assume that He has done so. This best of possible worlds necessarily can't be a perfect one; at best it will only have a balance of good over evil. Leibniz explained that although God is infinite, He has made a finite world, and the limits of finitude have to allow evil. Evil is thus an unavoidable ingredient. God accepts this as a risk He had to take. Even He could not fashion a world both finite and all good. Therefore, He produced the best world under the circumstances — the one we have.

Leibniz's theory became popular, but a half-century later it aroused the renowned French philosopher and man-of-all-letters, Voltaire, to write his savage satire, *Candide*. Leibniz's optimism inspired Voltaire to create one of literature's most endearing characters, Professor Pangloss. Throughout the novel, despite the harrowing misadventures of his pupil, Candide, Doctor Pangloss keeps insisting that we do indeed inhabit the best of all possible worlds. As a result, language is enriched by that wonderfully descriptive adjective, "panglossian," meaning ridiculously optimistic. In a letter to a critic, Voltaire attacked Leibniz even more bluntly. "When you have shown me," he wrote, "why so many men cut their throats in the best of all possible worlds, I shall be exceedingly obliged to you."

Neither Leibniz's boundless optimism nor Voltaire's scathing pessimism seems to provide a satisfactory answer to the question of why God allows evil. We get clues from them and from the story of Job's trust, from that stern idea of purification through suffering and from the divine contrast proposed by Thomas Aquinas. But the full answer still evades us. To get to the bottom of the enigma of God and evil, we must pose another question.

How can evil be good for us?

Evil, if it means anything, is that which is bad for us, and good is that which is good for us. Even to wonder whether evil could ever be good for us seems to pose a logical impossibility. After all, we should, and do, spend our lives trying to avoid evil. We don't want to bring harm upon ourselves or others.

But a Christian has to look at evil a little differently. There's no ducking it. Evil is here and here to stay. Bad things are going on all around us. If we believe in God, we have to believe that He created evil along with everything else. And we know we don't have to sin to bring evil upon ourselves. Evil happenings strike even the best among us. How can God be so unjust?

I think there is a real Christian answer to this puzzle, but it is a hard one to take in and perhaps an even harder one to live by.

The answer comes not directly from any one part of the Bible but from everything God has chosen to reveal to us about Himself, particularly through the life and suffering and death of Christ. The answer is that God allowed evil to exist. He did it for us. It is part of His great, free gift of grace, to bring us closer to Him.

Of course God could have made us all perfectly good — that is, perfectly like Christ — right at the beginning. And He could have protected us all our lives long from the evils that come with the natural laws of the universe. He could have kept us in perfect little Gardens of Eden, fully insulated from sin and all other dangers, where we would never have to work, never suffer, never be tempted to do wrong. Life would be a ball.

Or would it?

The rub, of course, is that there would be no temptation and so no free choice. We would not be able to sin, but we would not be able to love either. We would exist like well-cultivated vegetables, and our lives would be just as exciting as a vegetable's — and as meaningful.

So God has done something infinitely more wonderful for us. He has blessed us by allowing evil. He has allowed not just the evils we make by our own sinful, wrong choices, but all the natural evils of the universe. He allowed them for us, so that we can combat them and conquer them and come to Him freely after the battle, ready to love and be loved. God, in fact, has given us the only kind of love that can possibly count.

But why so much evil?

Couldn't God bring us to Himself with real love by means of a little less temptation and a little less travail? Couldn't He just as well have made the world a bit easier?

Perhaps. But He also could have made things a lot worse. All the evils we know could be infinitely more horrible. Hurricanes and earthquakes could batter us every day in the year. A tormenting, fatal cancer could eat slowly at every human body.

God, for our salvation, made the natural laws when He created the universe, and we can hardly expect the laws to change. But human beings endowed by God with free choice can effect change. Each age has its particular problems and benefits. A thousand years ago we knew less than we know today about curing physical ills, and, by and large, we cared less for the welfare and dignity of our fellow mortals. A thousand years hence we will have different problems and opportunities for different victories. The point is that in every age, the choices of men and women will create the changes; God's natural laws will stay unchanged and unchanging.

It is literally true, then, that we should not be resentful that God allows evil; for every effort and every right decision we make because of the evil all around us adds to the total of our victories and helps us toward our goal as Christians. God has set the conditions. He has created the battleground, the arena, where each of us must battle for our own soul. A Christian life isn't easy. God doesn't mean it to be.

The glorious fact, the central fact, of Christianity, is that the goal is worth all the effort and all the suffering and a lot more, too. With each day that we live, if we try to surmount the obstacles, if we try to help our sisters and brothers of all nations, if we try to make the world a better place, if we try to live by God's commandments, then we make ourselves better, bring our souls closer to God. In the process God helps us deepen and strengthen our faith and bestows His miraculous gift of grace upon us. This is what Christianity is all about.

We could never love God if we lived invulnerable and entirely secure, protected forever from ill fortune. God made us His creatures. He means that we should sally forth into the real world He has made for us and there find His true love and love Him in return. Only against a background of strife and struggle — and evil — can love be true love.

Why doesn't Jesus protect us from suffering?

Jesus' all-too-brief life here on earth was built on love. In the Gospels we discover a man who, in every sense, was all love. His compassion reached far beyond the norms of His day, even to the destitute and despised, down to the very dregs of society. Everywhere and to everybody, Jesus ministered and healed and loved and loved.

But today Jesus does not seem to protect you and me from suffering. Why?

We have decided God allowed evil here for a purpose and that we have to bear it. So is Jesus standing by, watching all this and doing nothing?

A good answer comes from the theologian Hans Kung. In *Does God Exist?* (Doubleday, 1978), Kung writes: "I can rebel against a God enthroned, above all suffering, in undisturbed bliss of apathetic transcendence. But not against the God who is revealed to me in Jesus' passion and all his compassion. I can rebel against an abstract justice of God…. But not against the love of the Father of the abandoned, made manifest in Jesus, in its unconditional boundlessness embracing also my suffering…making it possible for me to endure all the continuing distress and finally to be victorious."

Then Kung goes on to make a wonderfully perceptive distinction: "God's love does not protect me *from* all suffering. But it protects me *in* all suffering." God, says Kung, "is not a disinterested, unloving being whom suffering and wrong cannot move." Instead, He "has assumed and will assume man's suffering in love."

John Polkinghorne, who happens to be both an eminent scientist and an Anglican priest, presents the same idea in different words. In *Quarks, Chaos and Christianity* (Crossroads, 1996), he says: "One of my main reasons for being a Christian is that Christianity speaks to the problem of suffering at the deepest possible level. The Christian God is not just a compassionate spectator, looking down in pity on the bitterness of the strange world that he has made. We believe that he has been a fellow participant in the world's suffering, that he knows it from the inside and does not just sympathize with it from the outside. This is one of the meanings of the cross of Christ. Christians believe that God has shared our lot by living a truly human life in Jesus Christ.... He is not above us in our misery, but alongside us in its darkness."

So, yes, we humans are doomed to suffer, but along the way we will know plenty of joy, too. And no matter what the suffering, we can know that Jesus truly is right with us, right beside us, suffering with us every inch of the way. Our every pain, every sorrow, every disappointment pierces His heart, too.

And we might do well to ponder that if we love Jesus, we can suffer with Him, too. A century ago Charles Eugene de Foucauld left France for North Africa to lead an adventurous and ascetic existence as a soldier, explorer, monk, and finally, hermit. "I do not intend," he declared, "to go through life first class when my Master traveled third."

Perhaps the final word on Jesus and human suffering comes from St. Bonaventure, one of the great Scholastic thinkers of the 13th century. "Suffering," says Bonaventure, "is like a kiss that Jesus hanging from the Cross bestows on persons whom He loves in a special way."

If God has everything planned, how can we have free will?

In these questions and answers we have talked much about God wanting us to act voluntarily, to turn to Him of our own accord. But if an all-seeing God has the whole future mapped out already, how can we, His creatures, possess genuine free will?

Put it another way: Does God know in advance what each one of us will choose among all the choices we have to make through life? It's hard to see how He can know the outcome of anything unless He really does know ahead of time what we are going to choose. For instance, everything you choose affects somebody else. Your choice today to go to the store will affect what the storekeeper does and hence his choices and so on *ad infinitum.* Everything is thus one huge grid of interlocking choices stretching on forever. If God does not know how we will choose, how we will use the free will He has given us, He can not know the results and so can not know the future.

So it seems that although God gives us choices, He must know already what our decisions will be. Does He then also directly affect our choices, help us move toward one or nudge us away from another? If so, can we really describe these choices as free? And if so, why does God allow so many (apparently) bad choices?

Again, these questions tend to place God in a time box. You and I are locked into a time frame, but God is not. He is beyond time. Since God transcends time, indeed moves freely and simultaneously back and forth among past, present and future, there is no reason why He can't handle our decisions along with everything else. He is perfectly capable of giving us absolutely free will to make our own choices and at the same time fit the consequences of our voluntary actions into all the happenings of His Kingdom.

God knows everything there ever has been and ever will be all in one blinding flash of divine knowledge. So there is no contradiction between God's giving us free will and God's knowing the future. One way for us to understand this seeming paradox is to realize that for human beings there is a difference between free will and true freedom. God has given us free will to make the choices to keep sinning or to try to do better, to turn away from Him or toward Him. Only if we choose to turn to Him of our own free will do we feel the guilt of sin fall away. Only then do we find ourselves finally free, really and truly free, to love God. This is real freedom, the end product of what God wants for us. Thus, free will is only the means; true freedom is the end.

Martin Luther put all this in the form of another paradox: "A Christian man is the most free lord of all, and subject to none; a Christian man is the most dutiful servant of all, and subject to everyone."

Thus, we find true freedom through serving God. And one way to serve God is to serve our fellow humans. God is watching us. He sees us try. He sees us do the best we can, sees us take one stumbling step after another. We can be sure He is right here with us, encouraging us, holding out His loving arms.

How do I know I'm not just making God up in my head?

Philosophers like to talk about the theory of solipsism (from the Latin *solus,* "alone," and *ipse,* "self"). It means the feeling, which probably occurs to each of us once in a while, that we are the only real person there is and that everything outside ourselves is illusion. When you do get this idea, my advice is to forget it as quickly as possible and get on with your life. Yet the notion does have its attraction. After all, we can only be absolutely, rock-bottom sure of our own individual perceptions. I know what I feel, but I can only guess at what you feel.

Solipsism has nothing to do with one's personality. It can be felt the same way by a saint as by a villain, by a person with tremendous ego or by one with a huge inferiority complex. It has nothing to do with such modern vogues as "getting to know myself," "finding the real me" or "doing my own thing." It is simply a realization that I am me, a complete — and completely known – entity, and that, in the last analysis, everything else in the universe has to be taken on hearsay.

I think this deeply introspective feeling that comes to all of us helps to prove that God exists. How? When we look outside ourselves and see everything else that exists, we start to speculate. We can speculate that a jumble of atoms could have formed that sunset or that cathedral. We can believe that this random jumble could have created the words of Shakespeare or the music of Beethoven. We can believe that the jumble created our loved ones and – hardest of all – that the jumble even created the emotion of love itself. But I find that when I look back into myself, into my own mind, into the feeling of being pure me, then suddenly at this point I just can't believe in the jumble. I simply can't believe that my uniqueness, my feeling of pure me, comes from any accidental jumbling of atoms. I feel instead that there is Something guiding me, that this Something must have created me. I find I cannot look down deep within myself and not feel God.

Could my need for God just be psychological?

Maybe those promptings and urgings that we think come from God are really just our psychological needs. Emilie Griffin, discussing notable conversions to Christianity in *Turning* (Doubleday, 1980), comments that "it seems quite probable that God communicates to us where we are and through the dimension of our own emotional development." She adds: "And it seems quite characteristic of the God that I believe in that he would send to each of us just that sort of conversion experience which most deeply satisfies our emotional needs."

I find this idea challenging. We all have psychological needs that we might confuse with God's voice – the need for a father figure, the need to let some higher authority take over our problems, the need for comfort, and so on. Could it be that we are inventing God to satisfy these needs?

I don't think so. Sure, I have my needs, but I think God is real. The fact is God created us, and He also created all these needs we yearn to fulfill. So if in His wisdom He makes use of these feelings to reach us, so much the better.

The point is not to worry. God's word can come to us when we are quietly on our knees and looking to heaven. And it can come to us through our own tangle of fears and anxieties. Never mind. Either way, it's still God's word.

How do we know other religions aren't more real than Christianity?

We moderns sometimes think of the old-time believers as being so absorbed with Christianity that they overlooked the value of other religions. A good antidote is to listen to Basil the Great of Caesaria, a theologian of the 4th century. Nobody could have loved God more or studied harder to understand Him. Indeed it was Basil who took the lead in working out God's doctrine of the Holy Trinity. But Basil also had a huge respect for all other religions, and he gave us excellent advice. Don't condemn the faiths of others, Bishop Basil told his Christian flock, but, like the "honeybee," pick carefully what is profitable for your faith and reject the rest.

Each religion has its own way of picturing God. I am a Christian, so I have my particular way, but that doesn't mean I can't learn from others.

If I were a Muslim, I would believe there is one God and Mohammed is His prophet. If I were a Jew, I would be proud that my faith was the first to know that there is but one God and that we, the chosen people, paved the way for Christianity and for Islam. If I were a Confucianist, I would have all the laws of life laid out for me. If I were a Taoist, I would know the great Way of life leads straight before me, pure and true. If I were a Buddhist, I would strive to reach Nirvana and achieve ultimate reality. If I were a Hindu, I would try to earn enough good karma to break the cycle of incarnations and be swept into the Absolute.

All these religions are a treat for Basil's honeybee. Christians can profit much from them and, not least, we can discover that our Christianity has weaknesses. For one thing, we Christians tend to compartmentalize, keep our faith separate from the rest of our lives. Most of these other religions weave their faith into the very web of life, make their faith one with their culture. Christians can learn from them to put our beliefs at the center of our lives, to live our faith with our whole being.

But the study of other religions teaches something else. For a Christian – that is a believer in Christ – there is an emptiness, a loneliness, a profound sense of loss, in any faith that does not center itself on the once-and-only figure of Jesus. When we Christians pray, we don't turn inward, as do many of those who worship in the East. We turn outside ourselves to talk to a wholly personal God. As a Christian I believe that the One I talk to is no mere concept, no system of morality, no chain of incarnations, no Way of living, no Wheel of life. The One I talk to is a living God Who loves me and reacts to me. Indeed, I believe my God *is* love.

We of all faiths have different perceptions of God and we can all benefit from each other. Whose picture is more nearly right? All of us – Christians, Muslims, Buddhists, everybody – will know for sure when we get to heaven. Then we won't spend time worrying about whose guess came closest. We'll all stare in wonder and joy. We'll probably drop to our knees and gasp something like, "Oh, so that's how it is! My God, it's more wonderful than any of us could ever have believed!"

Why has God allowed so many divisions among Christians?

The doctrines of Christianity did not spring full-blown from the words of Jesus. The journey to defining what we believe has been long and tortuous. In the early centuries, the church's great ecumenical councils labored amid tremendous controversy and creativity to put the words of faith into creeds that could be affirmed by all. Along the way, heresies and schisms sprouted. The road to understanding the Christian message now has stretched on for two millennia. Halfway here East split from West, and this huge breach in Christendom has never healed. Again, halfway since then, reform – desperately needed but desperately divisive – caused the new Protestantism to break from Rome. Today, folk of good will are seeking union among all denominations devoted to Christ, but the road is still rocky and the end is not yet in sight. Distrust and intolerance thrive.

How long, O Lord, how long?

Is God up there watching Christians batter each other and doing nothing about it? Has Christ abandoned His followers who wallow in bigotry and hatred?

If we want an answer, we had better look at the clues of the last 2,000 years. First, Jesus could have made everything clear, could have spelled out all the doctrines Christians could ever need. But He didn't. He told us much, but He left lots more for us to puzzle out on our own. If we see through a glass darkly, it must be because God wants us to try to look for ourselves. We have the records of the Gospels, but human beings had to write them. We have the great insights behind the Epistles, but humans, still imperfect, had to find the words. We've listened to the great thinkers and preachers and leaders through all the years, but all have been human.

So, for the last 2,000 years have we been on the right track? Do we know more now than we did after Jesus ascended into heaven?

We can be sure that through the years God has been checking on how we've used the minds He gave us. In 325 A. D., when the Council of Nicea began grappling with the doctrine of the Holy Trinity, did God look down and smile and say, "Well, not quite"? A hundred years later, after the Council of Chalcedon, did He murmur, "There, that's closer"?

When Augustine sat striving to write a theology of Christ and the cosmos, God must have been looking over his shoulder. But did God nod His head yes or shake it no? When He heard Thomas Aquinas lecture on how to marry reason to faith, did God applaud or did He say sadly, "Not yet, my son"?

God has been listening to the modern philosophers, too, and we can be sure He has been merciful. But has He ever once been moved to exclaim, "There, that's it! You've hit it"?

We just don't know. It's been 2,000 years and we've seen much, but the glass is still dark. We can only believe that God must want us to keep following the clues, to search and to think.

And it's a good bet that God wants us to do something else. While we're wrestling with these daunting questions, while we're trying to figure out the message Jesus has left us, even while we're fighting for the doctrines we hold most sacred, we might try to exercise charity – Christian charity, that is – on those who differ with us.

Didn't the Apostles give us the final word?

The Apostles of Jesus knew the glorious blessing of hearing the Master speak to them in person. The rest of us have had to listen through the memories and explanations of others. Thus, the Apostles are our most basic witnesses. Yet we must remember that the Twelve who followed Jesus were humble men, fishermen, tax collectors and the like. Surely they told of their experiences, but it was the Gospel writers who put it all on paper, and the Epistle writers who tried to explain it. Since then, churchmen and teachers and theologians have worked over the centuries to bring us to a fuller understanding of those few, momentous, precious years when Jesus walked the earth.

The Apostles traveled far to spread the Good News of Jesus, and tradition tells us most of them met death as martyrs. We owe them a debt, and we are doubly fortunate that the generations immediately after theirs also produced brave and dedicated observers. Just as the right men were born at the right time to become Founding Fathers of our nation, so, too, with the Fathers of our Faith. From the 2nd to the 5th centuries, particularly, it seems almost as if God willed a select group of individuals, filled with an extraordinary measure of wisdom, eloquence and devotion, to set a course that would carry the heritage of Jesus down through the ages. But for the accidents of history some of the great works penned by these men could have been chosen for the canon to become books of the Bible. In any case, their accounts form a sequel to the New Testament, and the authors have become known as the Apostolic Fathers.

Who were these men? We have time only for a glimpse here and there. For sheer bravery we see Ignatius, for many years the bishop of Antioch in Syria, condemned for being a Christian and dragged by a guard of the emperor's soldiers to Rome. At any time during the long march he could have recanted. Instead, he wrote letters back to the faithful. "Here and now," declared Ignatius, "as I write in the fullness of life, I am yearning for death with all the passion of a lover. Earthly longings have been crucified; in me there is left no spark of desire of mundane things, but only a murmur of living water that whispers within me, 'Come to the Father.'"

Ignatius got his wish. About the year 107 A. D. he was flung into the Roman amphitheater and devoured by wild beasts.

His good friend, Polycarp, bishop of Smyrna, was condemned not to beasts but to fire at the stake. At age 86, standing in the flames, he thanked his God "for granting me this day and hour, that I may be numbered among the martyrs . . . now and for all ages to come. Amen."

Other Apostolic Fathers come down to us known not only for courage but for their insight. In the 2nd century, Justin Martyr was one of the first philosophers to try to reconcile Christianity with Jewish and pagan cultures; Irenaeus pioneered in explaining the theology of the pre-existence of Jesus as found in John's Gospel;

Tertullian brought a lawyer's skill to expounding the meaning of dogma; Origen wrote a monumental, point-by-point defense against those who attacked the Christian faith.

In the next three centuries, Athanasius fought to uphold "the-one-in-being" between God the Father and God the Son; John Chrysostom broke new ground in interpreting Scripture, and Jerome, living hermit-style in the Syrian desert, translated it; Ambrose of Milan raised the art of preaching to new heights; and perhaps the greatest of them all, Augustine of Hippo, developed an all-encompassing theology that helped form the bedrock of our faith.

The mission of all these men was to examine carefully the record left by Christ and the Apostles, then clarify their findings for the faithful. Their aim was never to invent; originality was the last thing on their minds. Read them, and not only faith but honesty shines through. They help us most of all because they followed so closely in the footsteps of the Apostles that they open a door into the past that we have all but forgotten, a past when our Christian traditions were being born. For a moment we can live as they did and feel the fervor of their newfound faith. The legacy of the Fathers is that they give us a priceless chance to peer backward through the corridors of time. Once we are there, we need look only a little farther to get back to Jesus.

How can Christian doctrine be true when it keeps changing?

"We live in a modern era – one in which there is an advance towards universal education. Men have hitherto depended on others, and especially on the clergy, for religious truth; now each man attempts to judge for himself."

That could have been written yesterday, but it wasn't. The writer was John Henry Newman and he wrote it 150 years ago. He went on: "Instead of looking out of ourselves, and trying to catch glimpses of God's workings, from any quarter, — throwing ourselves forward upon Him and waiting on Him, we sit at home bringing everything to ourselves, enthroning ourselves in our own views, and refusing to believe anything that does not force itself upon us as true."

Here Newman is cautioning against a trend that is even more prevalent today than it was in his era – the danger of losing the absolute truths of Christianity. Yet paradoxically Newman was also the great explainer of and apologizer for the idea that Christian doctrine, in order to preserve the great truths, must change. "To live is to change," he once wrote, "and to be perfect is to have changed often."

Newman's own career serves as a monument to change. Hugely respected as an Anglican leader and deeply attached to Oxford University, he bewildered his followers and sacrificed his friendships to become a Roman Catholic and eventually a cardinal. Newman's enduring legacies are, first, his eloquent expositions of the faith he searched for so diligently and, second, his perceptive, unshakeable conviction that Christian doctrine must keep changing.

The thesis of Newman's *Essay on the Development of Christian Doctrine* is that doctrine, far from being static, is alive, that it stems from Revelation, that it evolves through tradition, that it keeps evolving, and that it is the job of theologians and the church to keep it pure. This is true, he believed, not because great truths change but because the human mind needs time to grasp them. "The highest and most wonderful truths," explained Newman, "though communicated to the world once for all by inspired teachers, could not be comprehended all at once by the recipients" but have "required only the longer time and deeper thought for their full elucidation."

Newman held that this lengthy process, this rule of slow but sure development, has gone on throughout the history of human thought. In every field of knowledge we have expanded our insight century by century. Christian doctrine, he insisted, is no exception to this process. To understand, to try to probe the mystery of God, we should never be afraid to grow and to change.

So we are learning. We learned much during the early centuries of Christianity, we learned more a century and a half ago in Newman's day, and we are learning still. The hunt for truth goes on. In the 21st century we can be sure we will find brave new ways to explore and expound Christian doctrine. Every age has the duty to make the creeds relevant for its own time and to make God real for its own people. The challenge is to reconcile the facts of the past with the hopes for the future, to balance beloved tradition with bold initiative. To do so we must walk a high wire indeed. It's a job for all of us.

Why can't Christians agree whether God's Kingdom is already here?

A great mystery of the New Testament is the time for the arrival of the Kingdom of God. After the Ascension the Apostles seemed certain that the glorious new era promised by Jesus would start soon, perhaps any moment. Those men who lived closest to Christ passed their excitement on to the writers of the Gospels and the Epistles. The whole New Testament vibrates with expectation. It seems to proclaim that some tremendous event, something unimaginable, is about to happen.

Those first followers were convinced that the Kingdom of God whatever that might be – was just around the corner. The cataclysm might burst into our world next week, tomorrow, any hour!

Well, two millennia have dragged on, and the big moment hasn't arrived. I think the Apostles, although they tried desperately to understand the Master, must have misunderstood Him, at least in part. I'm sure I did. When I first read the New Testament straight through, that "about-to-happen" feeling overwhelmed me. I got hung up on a prophecy that failed. Christ seemed to be saying the Kingdom would come soon. And it didn't.

But what if, although most of us haven't noticed, the Kingdom of God already has arrived? If so, then my early reading of Scripture was too hasty. And maybe those Apostles were confused, too. The mistake could be the same for all of us. We haven't grasped the timing

103

of the Kingdom because we haven't paid proper attention to what Jesus told us.

The Gospel writers themselves seem perplexed not only about when the Kingdom would come but about what to call it. Mark and Luke speak of the Kingdom of God; Matthew prefers Kingdom of Heaven. John refers to the Kingdom only once, but he quotes Jesus emphatically: "Truly, truly, I say to you, unless one is born anew, he cannot see the Kingdom of God. . . . Unless one is born of water and the Spirit, he cannot enter the Kingdom of God" (3:3,5).

Modern biblical scholarship has added to the confusion. Almost everything Jesus said about the Kingdom can be translated or construed to be in either the present or the future tense. Is the Kingdom coming or is it here? Take your pick.

For instance, in one of Jesus' shortest and most familiar references to the Kingdom, He teaches us to pray, "Our Father Who art in Heaven, hallowed be Thy name, Thy Kingdom come . . ." Is He telling us to pray that the Kingdom will come? Or is He teaching us to acknowledge with gratitude and praise that God's Kingdom is already here?

Experts have pored over the grammar and idiom of ancient Aramaic, Hebrew and Greek. The more they study, the harder it is to choose between the present and future. Scholars have lined up on either side of the issue or sometimes plunked prudently down in the middle.

Those who maintain that Jesus meant the Kingdom has already arrived point to Luke 17:20-21: "Being asked by the Pharisees when the Kingdom of God was coming, (Jesus) answered them, 'The Kingdom of God is not coming with signs to be observed; nor will they say, "Lo, here it is!" or "There!" for behold, the Kingdom of God is in the midst of you.'" This would seem clear evidence for the Kingdom-now theory, but other experts contend that Jews of that day saw God reigning now in heaven and only later on earth. They insist that Jesus' mission was to prepare the world for the coming of the Kingdom.

Two other biblical passages that fuel the debate are: "Jesus came into Galilee, preaching the gospel of God, and saying, 'The time is fulfilled, and the Kingdom of God is at hand; repent and believe in the gospel!'" (Mark 1:14-15) and Jesus telling the Twelve, "Preach as you go, saying, 'The Kingdom of Heaven is at hand' " (Matthew 10:7). It's that little phrase "at hand" that causes the fuss. Some experts say it means the Kingdom is near, some that it is already here.

So much study by so many scholars. Perhaps, for a moment, we need to stand back and take a look at the New Testament as a whole. Put aside the nuances of language, the minutiae of meaning. Try to look instead into the depths of all Jesus' teaching. Can He be telling us that the timing of the Kingdom is twofold? Can He be saying that yes, the Kingdom is here, now, this very moment? And can He be saying also that, in another sense, a wondrous potential lies in wait for each of us in the immediate future?

The Gospel of Thomas is non-canonical, so Thomas or whoever recorded the book's sayings of Jesus is considered less reliable than the other Gospelers are. But

Thomas tells this about the Kingdom: "(Jesus') disciples said to Him, 'When will the Kingdom come?' (Jesus said,) 'It will not come by waiting for it. It will not be a matter of saying "Here it is" or "There it is." Rather the Kingdom of the Father is spread out upon the earth, and men do not see it'" (113).

I think Jesus must have said something very like this. He could have said it a number of times at different places with different phrases and images for different audiences.

In the total context of everything we are blessed to know about Jesus, He must be telling us that the Kingdom is indeed here on earth as well as in Heaven. But He must be telling us more. He must be telling us that something beyond our dreams, something so tremendous, so overpowering that it could turn us inside out, can also happen at any moment. He must be saying that when we are ready, each of us in his or her own time can grasp an opportunity and know a miracle. We can look within ourselves and there find God.

How can we know what Jesus thought of Himself?

Another great puzzle tantalizing biblical scholars is why Jesus called Himself "the Son of Man." Centuries of research have produced learned tomes and an abundance of ingenious theories, but the enigma remains. The experts have never reached a consensus. We just don't know what Jesus meant by this mysterious title.

In the four Gospels alone Jesus refers to Himself as "the Son of Man" some 80 times. If we could unlock this puzzle, find the meaning, we might learn more about our Lord and His mission. We might delve deeper into the core mysteries of the Incarnation: To what extent was Jesus conscious of His own divinity? Did He "remember" His pre-existence as the Logos, the Word? How, in fact, did Jesus view Himself?

What can "the Son of Man" signify? It does not appear to have been an idiom in common use in any language of biblical times. The expression does show up in the Old Testament, notably when Daniel recounts a dream where "one like a son of man" appears out of "the clouds of heaven" to rule the kingdoms of the earth (7:13-14). That vivid language may have been meant to portray the nation of Israel, and we have no real reason to believe Jesus used it for Himself.

The Gospels show that although Jesus spoke so often of Himself as the Son of Man, He never explained the meaning. It's possible the Apostles who heard the words from Jesus' lips were themselves perplexed. We have no record that they or anybody else used the title when addressing the Master.

One theory advanced by biblical scholars is that Jesus called Himself the Son of Man to emphasize His full humanity. Other students take an almost opposite tack. They think Jesus meant to point up His divinity, and the term thus gets twisted into something cumbersome like "the Son of Man Who is a God." Still others maintain the Son of Man in the mouth of Jesus is simply a circumlocution for "I," although they have never satisfactorily explained why such awkwardness would have been necessary.

Some modern experts propose a more complicated solution. They believe Jesus did not use the Son of Man to refer exclusively to Himself but rather employed it in a generic sense, as in "all of us," "everybody" or "anybody." They think Jesus may have found this useful to identify Himself with the poor and persecuted among His listeners. A problem with this theory is that such a roundabout speaking style hardly conforms to Jesus' usual straightforward eloquence.

Still other scholars have found an easier way out. They consider the use of the Son of Man so troublesome that they throw up their hands and deny Jesus ever said it. The problem is that these experts are equally at a loss to explain why the Gospel writers felt compelled to make up the phrase.

Well, 2,000 years is long enough to produce guesses, and it's beginning to look as if we may never know for sure what Jesus meant by the Son of Man. The scholars have had their chance, and now perhaps the rest of us should come up with ideas. I'm ready to make my own guess. This is not based on expertise but only from my reading about Jesus, my thinking about Him, praying to Him, listening to Him and being loved by Him.

I think Jesus called Himself the Son of Man because He loves us. He came to earth in human form to serve us by bringing us salvation. He came to serve all humanity, past and present. He saw Himself not only as a servant of God the Father but as a servant to us. He washed the feet of His Apostles. He died on the cross for us. He could have called Himself by that famous title used in the Old Testament's Book of Isaiah, "the Suffering Servant." But in talking to us, Jesus didn't stress "the Servant." Instead, over and over again, He kept calling Himself "the Son."

Why? Because He loved us, and loves us, so much that although He serves us, He feels closer to us than any servant could be. He is not only perfect God but perfect Man, and as such He is perfectly close to us. He is one of the family. He is a Son in the midst of us all.

Jesus sits at God's right hand and knows Himself to be, above all, the Son of God. But so infinite is His humility that, despite the enormous, overwhelming title of the Son of God, He also calls Himself the Son of Man. This very moment, in His eternal compassion, He is humbling Himself to be a Son even to you and me. Such is the measure of His love.

That's my guess. I'll let the scholars keep theirs.

Why do we need such a difficult doctrine as the Trinity?

The doctrine of the Holy Trinity is central to Christian worship, but it has fallen on hard times recently. Modern critics have been wondering why we need such a complicated formula as God the Father, God the Son and God the Holy Spirit. They consider the concept of a three-way God unneeded baggage to carry on the journey to a true and simple faith.

Some of those who question the value of the Trinity make the point that there is nothing in the Scriptures that directly spells out this doctrine. They note that the Apostles never heard of it and the Church existed for centuries without it. When the doctrine finally was formulated, they say, its function was not so much to declare a clear statement about God as to aim a defense against heresies. The critics contend that now that the heresies are dead, the Trinity has served its purpose.

But I think a closer look shows that it would be hard to understand Christianity without the idea of the Holy Trinity. We have to consider this: We believe in a God Who is, first of all, the Father Almighty, the Creator, the ultimate reality, the power back of everything, the One before all worlds and before all time. Second, He is the same God Who, while still being completely God, appeared on our planet 2,000 years ago and lived among us for some thirty years. He walked and talked and laughed and suffered as a full and complete human being — every bit as human as you and I. And third, He is the same God Who is acting right this very minute, Who

felt through us and through every ob-
____, Who is everywhere about us, and
____ght down inside each of us.

____e facts of Christianity, what the
____bout. They are the facts that God,
____ Jesus, made clear to us. They are
____rine worked out by mortal men
____ouncils. What the councils did,
____nd fifth centuries, was to take
____te a creed that would spell
____ the council members found
____ formula — complicated or
____n to us as the doctrine of
____aven't found any clearer
____tery of Christianity.

____omplicated is that we
____three Persons: Father,
____ looking at this is to
____an probably find at
____rson. Think of your
____you knew him as
____ts knew him in a
____p. Your father's
____ird way, and so
____but at bottom

I Want to Believe, but . . .
by Boyd Wright

The cover shows the stained glass window at the magnificent Wells Cathedral in Somerset, England, constructed from fragments of windows destroyed during the Reformation by those who considered representation of God in human form idolatrous. The shards were later reassembled into this non-representational form.
(From *Splendors of Christendom* by Dimitri Kessel, Edita Lausanne, 1964)
www.templegate.com

We, bein_____ begin to understand Go_____ ___ill never find the
right words to _____ ___ The best we can do is use
symbolism, an_ ___at's what the men who labored at
those early councils did. The creeds they drew up are

just that — symbolic ways of trying to get at the mystery of God. The councils came up with the Three-In-One and the One-in-Three. More modern theologians have come up with such ways of thinking about God as "Ground of All Being" or "Depth of Being" or "Being Itself." Those are symbols, too, images to help us grasp a truth we know we can never really grasp. Some of the modern concepts may prove helpful, but I think those old guys at the councils thought up the mental pictures that, over the centuries, have served us best.

How can we dare to think of God as a "Person"?

In our modern efforts to find new images to explain God, the personal nature of God often gets lost in the shuffle. It is precisely this idea of God as a Person that the early councils of the church managed to make clearer than have most of the up-to-date innovators.

With wonderful wisdom, the early churchmen chose the words "Three Persons" to identify the Trinity. Sadly, some people today want to scrap the concept of persons and substitute non-persons. Instead of God the Father, God the Son and God the Holy Spirit, they would have us pray to God the Creator, God the Redeemer and God the Sanctifier. If that brings them closer to God, I am all for it, but I think that if they lose the image of God as Person, they are losing the soul of Christianity.

Over the years, the concept of the Trinity has helped so much to bring me close to God that I would hardly know what to do without it. It has helped me because it has taught me to know God as a Person. Here's how:

First, when I think of God, and especially when I pray, my thoughts go upward, out of myself, to the ceiling or to the sky. There I get the feeling of God the Father of all, the God to Whom we pray, "Our Father, Who art in heaven . . ."

Next (not chronologically but somehow all in the same moment), my thoughts are back down to myself. I think of Jesus, the Man Who walked the earth with us. I think of Him right here, right now, sitting or kneeling next to me. He is so close that as I pray He is holding my hand.

Lastly (but again there's no shift in time), I am looking deep within myself. Here, right down in the depths of me, I find God's Holy Spirit. I feel Him acting in me, guarding and guiding me and filling me with His love.

That's the miracle of the Trinity for me. I send out three prongs of the same prayer, and I'm so used to it now, find it so natural, so necessary, that all three thoughts whirl though my head at once. There's no feeling of praying to Three; my mind is bent wholly to One. All at the same moment I feel the presence of God in three ways, above me, next to me and within me. It's that unfathomable, magical, divine formula of the Three-in-One and the One-in-Three that stirs my imagination and brings me to God.

Most important, the Trinity lets me know God as a Person. His wondrous Personality is so vivid, so alive, so real, that He is as close to me as anyone could ever be.

If Jesus is still with us, why do we need the Holy Spirit?

The Holy Spirit is all too apt to be the forgotten Person of the Holy Trinity. We have ways to visualize God, and we know Jesus to be a Man—but the Spirit?

The New Testament does give us a picture of sorts, a way to see the Spirit in our mind's eye. Chapter 2 of the Acts of the Apostles depicts the drama of Pentecost. Before Jesus ascended to heaven He had told His Apostles that God's Holy Spirit would come to direct and take care of them. Then, ten days after the Ascension, the disciples, seeking guidance, gathered in an Upper Room. Now, all of a sudden, this Spirit did indeed arrive, sweeping upon the faithful "like the rush of a mighty wind" and spurting "tongues as of fire."

That overpowering, almost savage, image is hard for most of us to sustain. Earlier, at Jesus' baptism, the Gospels had described the Spirit as descending "like a dove from heaven," and this gentler sign of peace may be easier to grasp.

The Spirit is not only hard to visualize, it has proved difficult to define. Theologians have come up with all sorts of ideas. They tell us He (or She or It) is God's love binding the Father and Son, and thus is the "responsive" Person in the Trinity; the sanctifier of our lives and souls; the energizer of the sacraments; the galvanizer of the Apostles and founding force of the church; the guiding light that illuminates the Scriptures and keeps our faith on course.

The Spirit has been called the Holy Ghost, the Paraclete, the Comforter, the Strengthener, the Counselor, the Advocate, the Inner Witness, the Giver of Life, the Breath of God, the Updater of Jesus. This Spirit is said to be at work always and everywhere and to act in manifold and mysterious ways. The Spirit puts charity into our hearts, impels us to sacrifice for others, makes us more like Christ.

St. Paul speaks much about the Spirit, and it may be he who gives us our clearest insight into the action of the Spirit. Paul even offers specifics. The Spirit, he says, produces "love, joy, peace, patience, kindness, goodness, faithfulness, gentleness, self-control." Paul goes on to tell us how to use these qualities. "If we live by the Spirit," he exhorts us, "let us also walk by the Spirit" (Gal. 5:22-25).

That may be as close as we can get to the true meaning of the Holy Spirit. Living by the Spirit gives us a prescription for living exactly that kind of Christian life that Jesus outlined for us. In fact, that's just what the Spirit is — a constant and comforting reminder that Jesus lives with us still.

But why should we pray to the Spirit?

Many of us find it easy to pray to God, to Jesus, even to Mary, but much harder to pray to the Holy Spirit. That's surely because the Spirit is so tough to visualize. Yet it's well worth an effort of imagination to try to reach this blessed but elusive Third Person of the Trinity.

If I search my own mind I come up with two pictures of the Spirit, neither of them at all like mighty winds or tongues of fire. First, I think of the Spirit as being throughout the universe in all things visible and invisible. This is an image of a kind of all-pervasive current of protective, soothing air. I get the feeling of something that fills everything everywhere, that doesn't stay static but flows gently around into everything and keeps flowing.

The second way I have of thinking about the Spirit is more important to my faith. I think of the Spirit as being right down inside of me. The feeling isn't exactly a warmth in my belly, and I can't pinpoint it in my heart or even my conscience. It's only a firm conviction that the Spirit is nestled deep in me, guarding and guiding me.

Now this feeling isn't altogether one of comfort. That comes into it a bit, but not as much as I might expect. It isn't at all a feeling that now everything has been taken care of and I don't have to do anything. The feeling is much more that I have hold of something infinitely precious for which I should be forever thankful

117

and that there is a great deal I can and should do in response. I feel that I want to hug this gift to me, care for it tenderly, nurture it, keep it growing.

If I truly search for the Spirit, I can feel a love welling up in me, a love for Jesus and for God, a love that somehow seems to grow into a love for my nearest and dearest, and from there out into a love for all mankind and for all that God has created. Yet this is a feeling not only of gratitude and joy but also of obligation. The Spirit seems to be prodding me to know what God wants me to do and wants me to be. The miracle is that the Spirit makes me feel God's presence.

I think I must have wasted years by not heeding the Spirit enough. The stupendous fact is that this is really God right here, right inside me. If I want to love God, I can let His Spirit lead the way. If I want to pray to God, I can reach Him through His Spirit.

But I must remember, too, that all this is mystery. The concept of the Trinity is finally and blessedly mysterious. If I hope to catch even a glimpse of God's Holy Spirit, I must practice true humility. I know there is a good reason I don't see the Third Person as clearly as I should. I listen to Jean-Pierre de Caussade, a devout, wise counselor who lived in the 18th century. The Holy Spirit, he tells us, "only communicates Himself to the humble, the simple, and those who are little in their own eyes."

Since God knows everything ahead of time, what good does prayer do?

It has to be one of the most baffling questions to face any would-be Christian. Theologians, who have wrestled with the dilemma from time out of mind, call it "the problem of petitionary prayer."

Problem? What problem? We pray to God for things we want, and we hope He answers. Sometimes He does and sometimes He doesn't. So there's no big problem, right?

Not exactly. The "problem" is one of logic, and it can bedevil a devout believer as much as an agnostic or atheist. The conundrum is that if we believe God to be all-knowing, then He knows what is going to happen in the future. So what good can our prayers do? How can we expect to change the course of events? Surely, we are not going to change the mind of an all-seeing, all-planning God.

This central problem brings up other theories about prayer. One is that God knows far better than we do what's best for us. You might pray for something God knows very well to be bad for you, so, in His mercy, He denies your petition.

Another fact about prayer is that it might have effects you could never have foreseen. If you pray for X to happen, it may not, but Y, something far better, may. If you pray that A and B patch up their marital problems and reconcile, they may not; instead they may get divorced and it may prove much better for both. If you pray for C to be cured of an illness and live, she may die — and go straight to a happier existence with God. If I ask God to help me fight my sin of anger, it may get worse, but all the while I may be conquering my envy.

Of course, we can never be sure if any of these results come from our prayers. But the very fact of praying implies faith and so implies trust. We must trust that God knows best — and we must keep talking to Him.

Yet that nagging question persists: Can my prayers — especially those particular pleas I offer up to God with every devout hope and trust and sometimes in real pain and desperation — really change any outcome?

I think those prayers can indeed affect events. First, of all, we must know God is merciful. He loves us and He suffers along with us, and it is inconceivable that He is going to ignore us in this or any other way. But beyond that, I think there is a valid reason — a reason based not only on trust and faith but also on logic — why prayers can make things happen.

We must tread carefully here. We know little enough about God and less still about His "knowledge." But consider this: God, since He is all-knowing and all-powerful, sees, or if you prefer has seen, everything there is, past, present and future, in one single divine instant of truth. God's knowledge does not come to Him, as yours and mine does, along a time line. He doesn't know one thing now, become aware of another a few seconds later, learn other facts tomorrow and find out more next year. He knows, or again if you prefer, has always known, everything there is, all at once, in that one blinding flash of knowledge.

We must keep in mind that this is at best a mental picture, one of those always inadequate attempts we humans must make to try to know God and His ways. But let's travel a little further.

Now, since God knows everything ahead of time, one of the things He knows is the outcome of what you are praying for. But God equally knows something else. He has given you free will, yet in His infinite knowledge, in that one divine instant, He also knows exactly when you are going to pray and what you are going to pray for. Thus God's knowledge both of your prayer and of the result of the prayer have always existed simultaneously. We could even put it that both the prayer and the outcome "came to God" at the same moment. This means that your prayer does indeed count for something. God, in fact, has "factored in" your prayer and meshed it into the whole scheme of things that is unfolding.

We mere humans can never hope to probe the mind of God, but I think that if we work through "the problem of petitionary prayer" with both faith and logic, we come up with a blessedly comforting answer. We can be sure that real prayer produces real results.

How can we know God is listening?

It may seem that sometimes we can pray and pray and pray . . . and it all seems to be going into a vacuum. How can we know God is listening? How can we know He is even there?

The late Dag Hammarskjôld, Secretary General of the United Nations and winner of the Nobel peace prize, must have had some such thoughts when he wrote, "God does not die on the day we cease to believe in a personal deity, but we die on the day when our lives cease to be illumined by the steady radiance, renewed daily, of a wonder, the source of which is beyond all reason" (*Markings,* Knopf, 1964).

If we don't hear God when we pray, perhaps one thing we can do is talk a little less and listen a little more. If we truly bend our mind to God, we may indeed hear something. That is the essence of prayer. It isn't just asking. Prayer is a two-way street. We talk to God and He talks to us.

Of course, we have to go about the task of prayer properly. Throughout the ages, mystics have set all sorts of examples from fasting, to wearing sackcloth and ashes, to praying to God while lying on a bed of nails. God may praise such extraordinary devotion, but chances are that from most of us He expects nothing of the sort.

I think God wants us to come to Him just as we are. And I think that when we pray, it helps to think of our prayers as working on three levels.

On the lowest and most basic level, we are taking our problems to God. These are our problems and they are uppermost in our mind. We want to tell God about them, and so we should. Prayer helps us mull the facts and think straight. If we are bothered by a particular problem and we take it quietly to God, the very fact of doing so clears our mind and makes us receptive to ideas.

On the second level, as we wrestle with this particular question, the ideas start coming in. Perhaps we can never be sure which of these thoughts bubble up from our own brain and which might be messages from God. But maybe that isn't important. What matters is that we are talking to God, really having a dialogue, discussing the issue, getting closer to Him. We have to tell Him our worries and we have to listen. The listening is the hardest part. But if we listen enough, I think we're bound to hear something. And if we listen very, very carefully, we may even learn what God wants us to do.

The third level is the least practical but the most important. If as Christians we believe that this life, as vital as it is, is but a flash compared to the life hereafter, we must also believe that everything we do here is really preparation. Every decision we make all our life long, the big ones and the little ones, does something that reaches to the very core of ourselves. Every judgment we make turns our soul a little bit away from God or a little bit toward Him.

God gives us free will and we have to make the choices. In the daily bustle of life we have to weigh what we must do in every situation that we confront.

Then, when we decide and when we act, we turn away from or we turn toward God. Every move is a step toward the life hereafter. Our decisions right now determine whether in the end we will be separated from God or whether we will live with Him forever.

That's what prayer is all about. We have to bring our problems to God. We have to talk with Him about the decisions we face. And we have to listen. If we can work up to that third level of prayer, we don't need to worry if God is really there listening to us. We can be sure He is. We can, in fact, be sure He is looking down at us, loving us and answering our prayers by helping us turn to Him.

Wasn't Jesus wrong when He promised all prayers would be answered?

Jesus taught us much about prayer and He even gave us a model, the Lord's Prayer, to get us started. Here He is specific about the different parts of a proper prayer: praise ("Our Father, Who art in heaven, hallowed be Thy name, Thy Kingdom come, Thy will be done, on earth as it is in heaven"); a petition for necessities ("Give us this day our daily bread"); confession ("Forgive us our trespasses, as we forgive those who trespass against us"); and a petition to make us better ("Lead us not into temptation but deliver us from evil").

All this seems clear enough, but Jesus also presented us with two important and startlingly contradictory facts about prayer. There's no way to duck it: Our Lord appears to have contradicted Himself, and we have to try to understand why.

In Mark 11:24 Jesus declares straight out: "I tell you, whatever you ask in prayer, believe that you receive it, and you will." Matthew (7:7-8) and Luke (11:9-10) make the same promise: "Ask, and it will be given you; seek, and you will find; knock, and it will be opened to you. For every one who asks receives, and he who seeks finds, and to him who knocks it will be opened."

Again, nothing could be clearer. Jesus is telling us that if we believe enough, our prayers will be answered. But directly opposed to this promise we have the evidence of an incident in our Lord's own life — His prayer in the Garden of Gethsemane. Here, as we discussed in the question about Christ's humanity, Jesus Himself is praying, imploring God, "Let this cup pass from me." Yet Jesus, although surely He if anyone has perfect faith, does not get His prayer fulfilled. The cup does not pass from Him. He suffers and is crucified. In His desperate prayer He asks, He seeks, He knocks — and His petition is rejected.

This disparity between what Jesus says about prayer and what happens when He Himself prays has bothered many a believer. Even the great Christian apologist, C. S. Lewis, who has brought so many into the faith, found the question unanswerable. He became so concerned that he wondered in anguish, "How am I to pray this very night?"

I don't pretend to be wiser than C. S. Lewis, but I think I can work out an answer that satisfies my doubts. First, that wonderful, awful, heart-piercing prayer of our Lord in the Garden of Gethsemane is so far above the comprehension of us mortals that I think it would be presumptuous for us to take it as a model for prayer. That was God the Son praying to God the Father, a holy mystery entwined in the very deepest and most sacred depths of the Holy Trinity. I think we would be much better off to stick to what Jesus said when He spoke directly to us. If we ponder His words, we may find some answers.

When Jesus says that if we believe enough, our prayers will be granted, He may be telling us something more subtle, harder to grasp and even more important than first occurred to us. We may be missing the point if we think of prayer simply as a formula: believe, ask, receive. Jesus may be telling us what prayer means in our relationship to God. He may be saying that prayer is a dialogue with God, talking and listening to God, getting to know God. He may be telling us that prayer, for each of us, is something divinely special, that it is, in fact, direct, personal, one-on-One contact with God. He may be saying that when we pray, we must give ourselves — our needs, our wants, our secrets, our souls, everything — to God.

Jesus may be telling us the most vital fact of all about the results of praying. He may be saying that if we believe enough, if we pray enough, God indeed will answer our prayers in the way that counts most. Jesus may be telling us that the end result of our prayers will be that we will know God's love.

Why do we need to pray to Mary?

We can pray to God, and we can also direct our prayers specifically to Jesus and to the Holy Spirit. So why should we also pray to the Virgin Mary?

Christians throughout the centuries have found immense comfort in praying to the Mother of Jesus. On the surface, it's easy to see why. Mary is the very image of all that is tender and sweet and dear. She is the beautiful Mother who nourishes and loves her Babe and later suffers tragically to watch Him die on the Cross. She is such a wonderfully warm and holy figure that she invites our prayers.

Yet, on another level, one can wonder. Father, Son and the Holy Spirit are the Holy Trinity, all-powerful, divinely complete. If we pray to Them, surely our prayer needs are fulfilled. There can be no higher authority. Why then pray to Mary?

Part of the answer is that many Christians find it necessary to put a figure between themselves and the mighty members of the Trinity. We feel so naked before the majesty of God that we reach out for someone to help us, to prepare the way, to intercede for us. Mary, the beloved Mother of God, is exactly and perfectly just such a figure.

But this does not fully answer the question. God, being all-wise, knows our prayers even before we utter them. And we know His mercy is infinite. Does it make any sense then to go through an intercessor? Why not go directly to God? When we talk to God, does He Himself really want someone to come between us? To put it bluntly, couldn't praying to Mary be more a hindrance than a help?

Many Christians would answer emphatically that Mary helps. Our hearts go out to her as a blessed buffer between us and the almost unimaginable, almost unreachable ultimate Deity. Her love is no roadblock to God. Instead, she guides us to Him, giving us strength and comfort along the way. If we pray to her, we can feel more certain that we are sending our thoughts straight up to God. Mary makes it easier for us to pray.

Women have found Mary even more helpful than have men, surely because it is easier to confide one's innermost needs and hopes to a member of one's own sex. A positive effect of this has been to help keep the doctrines of Christianity pure. Just in recent decades, the welcome and much needed power of women's liberation has brought on an urge to turn to a maternal deity. This, however, is not true Christianity. Christianity is the religion of Christ. Jesus never left the slightest doubt about it: He gave us the image of God as Father, as male as male can be. As Christians, we must believe Jesus knew what He was talking about. But the yearning for a mother figure is natural and it persists, so God, in His wisdom and mercy, has given us the blessed, enduring solace of the Virgin Mary. We can come to her so easily, tuck ourselves into her embracing arms, burrow into her boundless compassion. She is Mother to us all.

Sadly, Mary has sometimes proved a divisive figure within Christianity. Some denominations pay her more attention, place her nearer the center of worship, than do others. This causes some of the others to fear that glorifying Mary can downgrade the Trinity to the point of idolatry. These worriers might do better to concern themselves less with the prayer life of others and instead examine their own hearts to see if there might be ways Mary can lead them more surely to God.

For myself, Mary has come to play a big role in my prayers. Rightly or wrongly — and this is purely personal and may help nobody else — I keep her for one purpose. I pray to her for only one reason. It has become a habit, and, dumb as it sounds, I promise not to "bother" her about anything except this one supremely important petition. I pray to Mary only when I pray for the health and happiness of my beloved wife.

I find this very personal prayer in no way diminishes my devotion to God. Mary, in fact, brings me closer to God and Jesus. When I talk to her, I know her Son must be listening. Her love flows into me, down into my deepest roots. It reminds me of the love of my own mother, and, miraculously, it blends with the love I'm blessed to receive from my precious wife.

Mary's love does something else for me. Her love is so maternal, so total, that it helps me understand that other, even greater love — God's manly, fatherly love, the love that forms the stuff of the universe, that sweeps everywhere, but lives, most of all, right within my heart. Mary helps to bring it there.

Isn't it blasphemy to pray to physical icons?

Whether or not to pray with the help of a tangible object like an icon or a crucifix or a statue seems to arouse combative instincts in some Christians. There are those who consider the practice blasphemous. They insist this denies God and is tantamount to worshiping the Golden Calf that Moses railed against. Others explain that they don't pray *to* the object but use it simply as an aid, a tool, to help them pray. They contend that the proper use of an icon can remind us of Jesus, focus our minds on prayer and help bring us surely to God.

The controversy goes way back. The Apostles and early church Fathers portrayed their Lord in words, not pictures. Only slowly did believers take up brushes and chisels to render a likeness of Jesus. What took so long? It was no lack of fervor; many of the faithful worshiped so devoutly that they dared not depict their deity. And it was this fear that fueled a furious battle of ideas in the eighth and ninth centuries.

The lineup was iconoclasts versus iconophiles. The iconoclasts were certain that the early Christians refrained from creating images because this could lead to idolatry. Paint a picture of Christ, they argued, and you are blaspheming because you show only His human side, not His divine side.

Not so, retorted the iconophiles. They drew a distinction between idols and icons. Never, they agreed, should you pray to an idol, a thing devoid of reality. But an icon, they insisted, stands for something real; so it can indeed stand for Jesus.

Gradually the iconophiles gained ground. Christians came to see that it was proper, even a duty, to portray our Lord by whatever means mortal talent and ingenuity could devise. This paved the way for the great flowering of religious art during the Renaissance and after.

Today prayer is more private than in those days and our tastes are more eclectic. Images and icons help some, not others. For myself, to my shame I can remember once looking at the use of holy statues and pictures with a disgracefully patronizing attitude. These objects are pleasant enough to look at, I would admit, but hardly useful for the prayers of a Christian who prided himself on a grown-up, thought-out theology.

My comeuppance came one morning years ago when I had been going through a period of spiritual dryness. My too-feeble faith had set me to worrying whether the Jesus of history could actually be divine. Did God really try to reach us humans by making something miraculous happen two millennia ago in Bethlehem and on Calvary?

Alone in our apartment with my doubts, I knelt by the bed seeking guidance. In a drawer of our bedside table my wife Jean keeps a small crucifix and a statuette of Mary holding the infant Jesus. On impulse I grasped the statuette in my left hand and the crucifix in my right.

Suddenly I knew the answer. One life right between my hands. God, the baby born of a woman, living one perfect human life right on through to God, the man, dying on the cross. Fully human and fully divine. Both were making themselves known to me, right here, physically in my grasp. It made such instant sense that my doubts washed away. I felt Jesus to be so close to me, so real, that I could never doubt Him.

That day my cold, all-too-logical brain had reached for an answer, and my heart found it between those two little icons. That moment by the bed on my knees started me on the road to a better understanding of faith and of prayer.

Later Jean bought me a tiny crucifix, and I carry it always. I also keep a harp angel by our bed and hold her to say a special prayer morning and night. On the lamp above my desk hangs another angel who plays a cello. I look up from my work, and instantly I find myself warmed by his wonderfully comforting smile.

I know icons work for me. That little crucifix in my pocket and those little angels really do help me pray. They help because just beyond them I can see God.

What do we mean by God's "grace"?

If you want to stump a theologian, ask what might seem a simple question: What is the difference between God's Holy Spirit when He dwells within us and God's "grace"?

You'll get plenty of hemming and hawing and probably a long-winded explanation, but when it's over you won't have learned much. The fact is that theologians have so much difficulty making this distinction that we can be tempted to believe they just don't know the answer. (Sometimes the subject can get so technical you'll hear about "actual grace," "efficacious grace," "habitual grace," "justifying grace," "sacramental grace," "sanctifying grace," and "sufficient grace," but all these are defined differently in different traditions and sects.)

Even if we go back to the most noted theologian of them all, St. Paul, we don't find much help. Paul seems to use the terms "Spirit" and "grace" pretty much interchangeably. And, to make things more confusing, he also tells us over and over that not only are the Spirit and grace within us but that Christ Himself is "in us."

Perhaps, if we get away from the semantics and back to faith, we might find these distinctions are not so complicated after all. The important thing to remember is that God's Holy Spirit and God's grace and Jesus are all alive and that all dwell within us.

We might make some headway if we define "grace" as that aspect or manifestation or task of the Holy Spirit inside us that helps us accomplish things. As such, controversy about how this works goes back at least to the fourth century when it pitted St. Augustine against Pelagius. Poor Pelagius has had a bad press because he opposed Augustine, one of history's most celebrated theologians. But Pelagius was a good man who tried hard to understand God and made a lot of sense. He probably was a monk and he came from Britain and traveled over Europe and on to the Holy Land, writing letters and talking to anyone who would listen.

Pelagius' idea was that God has given us a mind and that we should use it to make ourselves good. Everywhere this earnest monk saw sin, especially within the church itself. He insisted that we humans could pull ourselves out of this mire of corruption and that this was exactly what God demanded we should do. Everywhere he shouted his favorite slogan: "If I ought, I can."

It was an appealing idea. Through strict obedience to God we humans could command ourselves. We could seize our own sandal straps and lift ourselves out of the muck. We could really do it. We only had to try. We could throw off sin. We could wrestle with the devil. It was a new era, a time of hope. Humanity, if it dared, could reach heaven by climbing to God.

Augustine was in his 50s and hard at work as bishop of Hippo in North Africa. A quarter-century had passed since he had left a dissolute life to convert to Christianity. He had written his dramatic *Confessions* and completed his opus, *The City of God*. He didn't need to take on a new fight. But Augustine worried about the tremendous popularity the ideas of Pelagius were winning.

He spotted a fallacy, so he too started to write letters and pamphlets and preach sermons. He threw himself into the battle with all the strength of his twilight years.

Pelagius' fine notions about human beings were correct, Augustine agreed, as far as they went. Indeed God gave humans a mind and a will and wanted them to be used. But there was something missing in Pelagius' scenario of hope. Human beings, Augustine explained, can't do these things alone. In fact, humans can't do anything by themselves. They can act only because God lets them. And they can come to God only because God has put into each of us that powerful, priceless gift of His grace. God doesn't only teach us how to be good; it is He who allows us to do it.

Supporters of Augustine and Pelagius tried to stamp their opposing views on the minds of the faithful. Devout men grew bitter. Charges of heresy filled the air. But gradually Christians – first the common folk and later church officials – came to realize that the old traditions held the germ of truth. Believers harked back to the teachings of Jesus. They came to feel that Augustine must be right, that persons have free will to accept or reject God, but that if they do accept, they will find that God's grace acts within them.

The wisdom and faith of Augustine pointed the way. He knew that human will and God's grace, far from being opposed, complement each other. He knew that both are connected in a single process that heals and preserves the soul and that it is impossible to see where one ends and the other begins. He knew that grace acts through human will, not overriding it but guiding it.

Above all, he knew that both free will and grace are gifts for which we should be everlastingly thankful to God.

So Pelagianism swept to the rampart of our faith and was beaten back at the last moment, and Christianity, which might have been very different, is what it is today. But still . . . Do we really stand with Augustine? Or are we even now a little bit Pelagians at heart?

The answer, I think, is that we must seek to be aware of God's grace and to try to recognize it acting within us. If we feel it to be a part of the Holy Spirit, then we can be helped and guided to a better life. It's one more way to feel God's love.

Why do we need such a complicated formula as "atonement"?

If we examine God's great gift of grace a little more closely, we might discover a surprising fact: It is absolutely free! Just once in the universe there really is a free lunch. God has given us this gift with no strings attached. We have never deserved it. We have never lifted a finger for it. We don't have to be good to receive it. God has just handed it to us.

So what exactly is this gift? To try to understand it, the early Fathers and later some theologians tried to put the concept of the gift into a formula. Now formulas help some people but not others. If you are mathematically or scientifically inclined, you probably like formulas. If you have trouble with math, you probably hate them. But this one is a word formula and not really hard to fathom provided we define the words that make it up. The formula is this: *Atonement is justification by grace through faith*. To put it in a more mathematical mode, it would be: *Atonement = justification + grace + faith*.

Now for the definitions:

Atonement means at-one-ment. In theology it is the state of being at one with God.

Justification is the act of making just or putting to right or making righteous.

Grace is a great gift of God to us, an undeserved present that we have never earned by our own merits. It is God dwelling in us, enabling us to do things.

Faith in this context is our response to God: belief in His existence, trust in His goodness and gratitude to Him as shown by the life we try to lead.

Christians believe that *atonement* took place when Jesus hung on the cross and when He rose from the dead. It is what Good Friday and Easter Sunday are all about. The formula for atonement means that we are helpless sinners. We sin all the time and we can never come close to Christ's command to love God with all our hearts and souls and minds. So God has given us His *grace*, that great undeserved gift. When Jesus suffered and died, He did it for us, absorbing the pain of our sins into Himself. As the human Jesus, He thus made full reparation for our sins and won forgiveness for us. This way He *justified* our lives and reconciled us to God.

Now look back at the formula. That last factor, *faith*, is up to us. Atonement works only if we do three things:

(1) We must examine our consciences and truly repent our sins.

(2) We must have faith in God and truly trust His forgiveness.

(3) We must change our lives and truly try to overcome our sins and live as God wants us to.

The formula is a continuing process, and we can keep it going only if we let the Holy Spirit work within us. This means we must keep on repenting and keep working to make our faith strong.

Motive is important. As we discussed back when we answered our question about salvation, we are not striking a bargain with God. We are not saying I'll be good

139

so I'll be saved. The formula doesn't work if we are motivated only by wanting to earn salvation. Instead, we have to be moved by gratitude for that wondrous gift of grace already received. Then, as we let our thanks show forth in our lives, we find ourselves producing good works. Keep at it and we develop habits of gratitude and goodness. And these, we can be sure, will lead to the habit of happiness. For the formula is finally complete only when we know the perfect joy of being at one with God. That's what *atonement* (at-one-ment) is.

There we have the great equation worked out by Christian believers. It's tougher than any of the formulas of science or math most of us had to learn in school. It's tougher to believe: How can it be that we have a Savior so merciful, Who loves us so much that He hands us this undeserved gift? And it's even tougher to live by: How can I give enough of myself to God to keep the formula working?

The answers aren't easy. To make it all work out, a good start might be to get on our knees and ask God's help. His love will help us find the way.

Original Sin? How can God be so unfair?

The concept of Original Sin has to be one of the most baffling to confront any believer. I know. For years I insisted it just didn't make sense. God is loving, and He certainly must be fair. So how can He possibly hold us accountable for sins committed by our remote ancestors?

The doctrine comes, of course, from the Genesis story of Adam and Eve. We discussed this myth when we talked about the problem of evil, and now it teaches another lesson. God told these first humans not to eat from the Tree of the Knowledge of Good and Evil, but they disobeyed and so were banished from the Garden of Eden and sentenced to all the hardships of life. Adam and Eve stand for Everyman and Everywoman. As their descendants we are supposed to keep suffering for their sins.

I used to be perplexed why Christians took this myth so seriously. Surely they must have been interpreting it the wrong way. An all-merciful God would never allow such illogic and injustice as to make us pay for others' mistakes. Yet after years of mulling the story, I've come to the conclusion there is a good bit of truth to it.

Maybe the concept of Original Sin is easier to grasp if we forget Genesis for a moment and substitute other images. Try this: God didn't start off by making a pair of humans and putting them into anything like a perfect Garden of Eden. What God did, and does, is make humans, all of us, morally neutral. That is, He gives us

141

bodies and brains but He doesn't build into us any moral direction, any sense of right and wrong that can guide us beyond our own reasoning. In effect, he launches us on the voyage of life without any moral compass.

So we start out neither good nor bad and with nothing in us that steers us toward sin or away from it. Our human nature takes over and we follow our instincts, to feed and breed and survive, to think of number one, to do those things that help ourselves, not others. But we have the brain God gave us and wants us to use. And each of us learns that anarchy is not the best condition for me, for number one. We find that life is much easier for each of us if we make rules. So our ancestors pooled efforts to bring down the prey and share the meat that the tribe killed. Now we draft laws and put up traffic lights and develop morals and a whole code of ethics. But we do these things not because God planted any sense of right or wrong in us. We draw up the rules for all because the brain in each of us tells us this is best for number one.

That, for me, is Original Sin. At this point we are still in our original state. It is the state that animals stay in, that babies are born into and that some people, I'm afraid, never grow out of. But there is something beyond this, and that Something is God. We leave the state of Original Sin by turning to God. We do it not because He has implanted direction in us but because we turn to Him, choose Him, through our own free will, through the free will He has handed us as a gift.

From living in Original Sin, each of us learns about God from others, from reading and thinking and praying. We are free to decide and to choose. Then, when and if our brains and heart – our free will – let us believe, we turn to Him. And at exactly that moment a strange thing happens. Each of us is no longer number one to ourselves. God is Number One. And once we know that, a second miracle happens. God is Number One and suddenly our loved ones are number two and number three and other people we know are numbers four and five and those who are almost strangers are number six, and we find ourselves, who were number one, so far down the list we might as well be number x.

In a moment our whole world has turned upside down. We are looking at things from a completely new perspective. We have passed out of Original Sin.

This doesn't mean we are not going to sin any more. Temptations lurk everywhere, and we still love the old number one much more than we should. But now we turn to God and He shows us how to live a better and a happier life.

Anyway, that's my myth. Maybe it's no clearer than that of Adam and Eve, but it has helped me. I do believe I once lived in Original Sin and I do believe I feel better now.

The story, of course, is not finished. What I have been trying to explain to myself is an Old Testament concept, but I know from the New Testament that the best is yet to come. I know that any Original Sin and all my sins are forgiven because God sent Christ Jesus into the world to save me. That is the perfect joy of being a Christian.

Can we believe in both God and science?

Religion versus science. Faith versus reason. To us moderns these pairs often seem diametrically opposed, mighty forces of knowledge forever set on a collision course. But it was not always so. For centuries science and religion marched side by side, the same great minds seeking answers to the same riddles. They parted only in the 17th century with the dawn of the Age of Enlightenment. For over two hundred years they have gone separate ways, but right now they seem almost to be coming together again.

Why? Perhaps we are entering an era of ever more enlightened Enlightenment. In any case, scientists, particularly cosmologists, physicists and biologists, are paying more heed to what may lie even beyond conventional science. And scholars of the "softer" disciplines, including philosophers and theologians, are meshing their studies more and more with science. These days everybody seems to be trying harder to learn from others.

There is even some crossing of careers. Take John Polkinghorne, who spent twenty years as a particle physicist, becoming a professor at Cambridge University. Then he left physics to take orders in the Church of England and became president of Queens College, Cambridge. He points out that both science and religion are "concerned with the search for truth." But there is a difference. "Science is essentially asking, and answering, the question 'How?' ... Religion, essentially is ask-

144

ing and answering the question 'Why?'" Polkinghorne says that as a result of both his careers he has come to realize that "in the realm of personal experience, whether between ourselves or with God, we all know that *testing* has to give way to *trusting*. Faith may involve a leap, but it's a leap into the light, not the dark." *(Quarks, Chaos and Christianity,* Crossroads, 1996).

Today theoretical scientists rank two related puzzles as the greatest quests in the search to explain the universe. The first is to find a grand unified theory of energy, that is to unify the four known categories of force. The second is to discover a quantum theory of gravity. This means reconciling Einstein's theory of relativity with the quirky, unpredictable and still emerging field of quantum mechanics. These two pursuits have helped change the face of science.

It used to be that to settle such great cosmic questions astronomers searched the heavens while physicists, chemists and biologists holed up in the lab to study minutiae. Now the men and women behind the telescopes and microscopes are one. They look both way down and way up to probe the origin and map the destiny of the universe. They spend time at the same blackboards working out the same formulas. They track masses that hurtle through space and specks that whirl on a pinhead. Nothing is too big or too small. Gulliver has finished his travels and come home.

The new scientists are working with the philosophers and the theologians. They are weaning us away from a purely reductionist concept of the universe toward a more holistic one. They are not just tearing everything apart to get at the basic building blocks; they are standing back, looking not only at the parts but also at the whole, fitting the jigsaw pieces into the big picture. They are finding that while the world at one level is a collection of connected concrete objects, at a whole different but complementary level it can best be understood as a vast network of intangible but interacting relationships. This broader, calmer perspective may just be the way to uncover some of the truths that have evaded us in our headlong rush to progress. Stand back far enough and take it easy enough and we may get a better view not only of creation but also of the Creator.

Hasn't science already debunked God?

God has revealed Himself to us only through that mysterious process we know as "Revelation." Apparently He wants us to come to Him by faith alone, and He has made it impossible for us to "prove" Him. We will never glimpse God on a photographic plate or discover signs of Him in a chemical sample. But God, despite all the efforts of doubters and cynics down the ages, is also impossible to disprove. The best scientists know full well that a boundary of knowledge exists beyond which science cannot reach.

Today scientists and theologians more and more are using the same tools to ply their trade. As science grows more complicated and specialized and harder to explain to laymen and even to other scientists, the scientists themselves have turned to the techniques we who try to explain God have been using since Biblical times.

We Christians draw pictures to show how we perceive God. Sometimes we sketch actual pictures, portraying clouds to show heaven or circles to explain the Trinity; sometimes we create pictures with words, as when we tell the myths in Genesis or the story of Job. We know these images are necessarily imperfect, even crude, but they are the best we can do to express something unimaginable and unexplainable. Now scientists, as their studies get harder and harder to visualize and some of their subjects get tinier and tinier, have taken to the same tricks. They draw diagrams to show such things as the innards of an atom or the hungry maw of a

147

black hole, but they know the descriptions they invent are just that, pictures or representations.

For instance, one modern theory holds that the universe is finite but has no boundaries or edges and so curves back around itself. To describe this cosmologists draw something that looks like an inner tube or a doughnut. Everybody realizes this is a concept, not a real shape. On the subatomic level, even some particle physicists have given up picturing particles as particles; instead they are sketching strings. Precise science, like her vaguer cousin religion, is forced to speak in metaphors. Niels Bohr, the father of quantum theory, has put it: "When it comes to atoms, language can be used only as poetry."

Quasars and quarks and protons and probability waves don't really look like the pictures of them, but to understand them we have to glimpse them in our mind's eye, no matter how inadequately. To grasp them at all, to work with them, we have to hold onto an image.

So with the images we have to use to try to understand God and to try to make sense of ideas like grace and atonement and the Holy Spirit. Science teaches us that things don't always have to be seen to be real. Those who debunk God are fond of saying He is just in our minds. Well, in a sense an atom and a black hole exist only in our minds, too. We will never see them. They are only pictures, but they are pictures that represent something completely real. We can't see an atom, but if it weren't here, we wouldn't be here either. We can't see a black hole, but if we got sucked into one, we would know it soon enough.

We can't see God either, but that doesn't mean He doesn't exist. In fact, we may be able to use some scientific insights to get to know Him better.

But can science ever help us understand God?

Our expanding knowledge of the universe is actually bringing us closer to an understanding of God. Let's try stretching our modern awareness of the physical world to see if we can come to any conclusions. Consider just three facts:

(One) The fact that the sky swarms with billions of stars, perhaps surrounded by billions of planets and moons, worlds upon worlds stretching into boundless space for billions of light years; that even this is not what we can envision as infinity, but that the whole giant universe could be a speck nestled into a bigger one, and that could be nestled into a bigger one, and so on; and that this seeming infinity could crunch downward, too, with a tiny universe nestled into a single speck of the air I am breathing right now, and a tinier one could be nestled into that one, and so on.

(Two) The fact that inside each cell of each of Earth's living organisms are complex strands of replicating DNA that provide not only the spark of mortality but spell out enough detailed instructions to program centuries of life.

(Three) The fact that you and I, human beings, can sit here thinking about these things.

Put these three facts together and it's tough to believe that all this results from an accidental scramble of atoms. It's hard to believe there isn't something like a

Supreme Cause, something very like God, behind it all. This may not be proof, but it's a pretty good pointer.

Isn't our way of looking at God out of date?

Every age considers itself wiser than those that came before. We today want always to be modern, to seem to be with it. Even we Christians, whose faith centers on a miracle that happened two thousand years ago, are always trying to change things, an urge C. S. Lewis once called the "liturgical fidgets." Numberless millennia from now, even if only two Christians are left, one will probably turn to the other and ask, "How can we make Christ more relevant for today?"

Change, of course, can be good. We have to try to use all our skills and knowledge – and our prayers – to find new ways to understand God. But if we want to keep our perspective as to what Christianity is all about, it might be worth taking a quick trip through time. Start with that simpler age when people believed God came down and meddled in human affairs. When He was angry He stirred up floods and plagues; when He was gentle he made laws, cured ills, sent angels as messengers and sometimes appeared in visions.

Then came science, and humans learned that laws of nature run the universe. Those were never really miracles; they were orderly results of orderly causes, all easily explained by the new-found rules of meteorology or biology or psychology. So believing became harder. The believers had to say okay, God didn't actually intervene every time, but He made the laws that set off those reactions that made the "miracles." Back of everything there is still God. He started it all.

Then, just during the 20th century, that position has crumbled, too. Science tells us God didn't even have to meddle to create the universe. It was all explainable, natural science. The universe began with the Big Bang. We can even pinpoint it some thirteen billion years ago. We know just what elements touched it off, how hot and how dense they were. We can measure how fast the cosmos is expanding and even compute how it might some day contract.

So be it, said the believers. The laws of nature did all that and God didn't have to intervene. But He did something far greater right here on this planet: He struck the spark of life – and science can never explain that.

But now, of course, science has. In the last few decades molecular biologists have shown that those same laws of nature did indeed start life. Mix proteins with the right nucleic acids and presto you get organic matter. If the mixture has the right DNA's, it can reproduce itself and make other single-celled living things, and they can become bigger and evolve through the survival of the fittest into even stronger and more complex creatures and become mammals and men and women. Before you know it, you have produced the mind of a mathematician and the heart of a saint, and nature did the job all by herself.

But the faith of the true believers holds firm. They know science is going to spring more surprises. It will press on to course the galaxies, to find a grand unified theory of force, to unlock the mysteries of quantum mechanics, to grasp the secret of how our own brains work.

I think that as we peel away marvel after marvel, work closer and closer to the core of knowledge, true believers will make another discovery. They will find their faith not weaker but stronger. With every step they will become more certain that now and forever, beyond all, back behind everything, there is God.

How will they know? Because right in the middle of this long march of events came a happening so momentous, so meaningful, so real, that its transcendence stretches both backward and forward through all time. Christ came into the world and lives with us still.

Christianity is not a religion of theories and of comfort and of good will. It is a religion of history and of fact. When an event has happened, it has happened. All the vast reaches of time, of infinity itself, do not change what has gone before. A fact stays a fact.

To be a Christian is to believe the fact of Christ, the facts of His life and death and the fact that He is with us now. We don't need only to seek fresh concepts; we need to understand the old ones better. We need to treasure and study every one of those precious, illuminating years when Jesus trod the roads of Galilee and Judea. We need to shine new light on His teachings and find ways to lodge them into the depths of our being. We need not so much to grope for the new as to remember the past and make it so real that it works for us today.

He Who brought the Good News is forever and perfectly new. If we look back hard enough to what He was, we will see what He is right now. To know Jesus is to know that He does not change.

We Christians must stand ready to meet new challenges. We must be creative, stretch ever higher to find new ways to worship and to strengthen our faith. We must live fully in the present and look hopefully to the future. But we must remember we are indeed Christians. Always, we must stay focused on Christ.

Are we humans really so special?

Scientists seem to be talking more these days about the Anthropic Principle. The word comes from the Greek *anthropos*, meaning "man." The idea is that the composition of this planet in particular and the universe in general, the conditions of density, humidity, temperature, climate and the like, all fall within such a narrow range, are all held in such a remarkably delicate balance, that they must be designed to create and sustain life, especially human life.

The theory contends that the Big Bang itself must have been primed so precisely and aimed so accurately down the eons that it ignited the chain of evolution and in the end generated intelligent beings. From this the proponents conclude that behind this great drama there must have been a Primer and Aimer, in fact a Creator. They maintain that this not only proves God exists but that we humans are here because He devised the whole cosmos to produce us.

I don't think much of the Anthropic Principle. I don't think it proves the existence of God, and I don't think it tells us much about ourselves. Isn't it more plausible that the advocates of this principle have got things backward? This hardy little germ we know as life, this mixture of proteins, nucleic acids and DNA's, has endured the buffetings of nature and is hanging on with the tenacity of a pit bull. I think it much more likely that instead of the environment being shaped for life that this tough little spark of life has adapted itself to the particular conditions that prevail here.

I also think it likely that on other planets, where heat and cold and gases and winds swirl about in ways unimaginably different from ours, there, too, life or something like it has managed to gain a foothold. This kind of life may have accustomed itself to whatever weather and hardships are there and may flourish in forms we could hardly recognize. If so, the Anthropic theory fails. If we humans don't stand at the center of all, no need for a divine Creator Who planned everything around humanity has been demonstrated.

I'm afraid the tendency among too many Christians is to put humans on a pedestal. We don't belong there; God does. The Anthropic Principle glorifies humankind, and we don't begin to deserve it. Sure, God created us to love and to be loved by Him. But that doesn't make us unique in the cosmos. We are not alone. God, in His infinite love, may care just as much for beings, either more or less advanced than we, inhabiting other planets in other galaxies and other worlds in other universes.

We humans must learn to think of humanity with humility. The Anthropic Principle is not for us. The real principle behind the be-all and end-all of everything points not to humankind but to God. His love is indeed infinite. And it may not be aimed only at us.

What about all the great thinkers who have put God down?

Philosophers over the ages have come down both for and against the truth of Christianity. Sometimes we tend to think that the early thinkers, weighed down with superstition, were more in favor of God and the metaphysical, while more modern philosophers take a harder, perhaps more realistic, look at things. That isn't so. Take, for instance, a Platonic scholar named Celsus, who wrote a systematic attack on Christianity as early as 180 A. D., barely a century and a half after the crucifixion.

Celsus asked tough questions. How can we be sure of the Resurrection? How do we know Christ rose from the tomb on Easter morning? Aren't we just taking the word of a hysterical woman and a few deluded disciples? Maybe those desperate followers of Jesus imagined the whole thing or made it up.

Then Celsus tore into the logic of Christianity. If a god came to earth, why couldn't he save himself from torture and death? "How could we regard him as god when he . . . was caught hiding himself and escaping most disgracefully and indeed was betrayed by those whom he called disciples? . . . One who had eaten a banquet with a god would not have become a conspirator against him."

Celsus was no hasty critic. He showed a profound knowledge of pagan myths and Greek philosophy. He believed in a monolithic God, but he derided the basic premise advanced by Christians. "A god would not have had a body such as yours," he declared. If the true God "did wish to send down a spirit from himself, why did he have to breathe it into the womb of a woman?" And why just "into one corner" of the world? God "ought to have breathed it into many bodies in the same way and sent them all over."

The whole time frame of the Jesus story is ludicrous, Celsus insisted. "Was God then unable to correct men merely by divine power, without sending someone especially endowed for the purpose?" And why at that moment in history? Did God "not care before?"

Celsus saw nothing novel in the chronicle of Christ. He dismissed the myth of a hero dying then coming back to life as being as old as mankind – superstition told to "gullible people." Christians, he complained, refuse to give reasons. Instead, they say, "Do not ask questions; just believe."

Celsus is particularly rough on the apostles, branding them scoundrels, fools, wishful thinkers and hallucinators. Jesus, he says, surrounded himself with "sailors and tax-collectors of the most abominable character." These, he notes, did not die with their Lord and later "even denied that they were disciples." Nor does the Virgin Mary escape attack. Celsus charged she was "turned out by the carpenter who was betrothed to her, as she had been convicted of adultery."

We can be sure that in his scorn for Christianity Celsus was not alone. He was, in fact, a deeply cultured conservative who flailed Christianity because it threatened what he held dear. He feared that the fresh wind of this vibrant, new religion might sweep the ancient cherished traditions away forever. And he was right.

For us, the legacy of Celsus is that criticism of Christianity — even the most severe debunking — is nothing new. It goes on today, but it started back when our faith was barely born

Seventy years after drew up his diatribe, Origen, an eminent scholar of the early church, offered a rebuttal. Christ as the Logos has always existed, explained Origen, but God came down to earth as Jesus at a particular time and place for a particular reason. Precisely then the Logos united with a human soul and body, and the purpose was nothing less than the salvation of all people before and since. God becoming man did not diminish God; it liberated us.

Further, declared Origen, it is exactly this redemptive purpose that explains why Jesus refused to use divine power to avoid the cross. Only by joining Christ in death can we be born to new life. In those incredible tales of the first Christians, Origen could hear the ring of truth. Why, he asked, would the apostles discredit themselves by inventing the treachery of Judas and the denials of Peter?

Two centuries after the crucifixion Origen could point with pride at those friends of Jesus who Celsus was so sure had failed their Master and flimflammed the world. Those same disciples had faced the hells of persecution to shout the Good News everywhere. And even the bravest of men, Origen concluded, don't die for lies.

A century later another great churchman gave another answer. Athanasius was a bishop so resolute that he endured exile five times and so holy that his name adorns one of our creeds. He defended the reality of the resurrection by demanding: "Is he a dead Christ who even now is revolutionizing the lives of men?"

Maybe Origen and Athanasius said it all way back then. Maybe we haven't come up with any better answers. But be of good heart. Celsus shows us that for 1,800 years the doubters and debunkers haven't come up with any new questions either.

Haven't later philosophers discredited Christianity?

Examples of faith keep springing up in the most surprising places. Take two philosophers, one English, one German, who changed the thinking of their respective eras and are still listened to with respect today. Both were as tough, as no-nonsense as you can get. Nobody ever accused either of abandoning reason for sentiment or piety.

Thomas Hobbes (1588-1679) has to be one of the most materialistic philosophers ever. He was considered such an atheist that in 1666 a jittery English Parliament banned his books. Some nervous M. P.s feared Hobbes' freethinking ideas had alone been responsible for bringing down God's wrath to cause the Great Plague and the Great Fire of London.

Hobbes wrote widely on political theory and mathematics and pioneered in the field of analytical philosophy. His central idea was his insistence that the world is run solely on the rigid rules of cause and effect. This is where his critics sniffed atheism.

But Hobbes, although a materialist to the bone, was far from an atheist. What his detractors failed to notice was that he kept following the long, long chain of effects infinitely backward. Where do we end? There is a point, Hobbes came to believe, where material things stop and we have to use a different method to work back to an original cause. How? By the method of faith.

Read Scripture, Hobbes said. There is nothing there contrary to reason. God is there, and Jesus Christ is the Son of God. But by what authority do we know?

Right here our philosopher took a giant leap. We can almost see him lay down the tools of mathematics and analysis, and look upward for guidance. We know, Hobbes concluded, because we have a friend, and we can trust this friend just as we have learned through experience to trust our other friends and loved ones. This friend is Jesus Christ.

It comes down to trust. Jesus in the Gospels told us of the Father. And the Father, if you go back and back through all the links in the chain of causes and effects, is the explanation for the universe.

So at the end of the trail Hobbes found faith. We can rejoice that he also found fulfillment in his personal life. A royalist during the English Civil War, he was exiled to France and there tutored the young son of the beheaded King Charles I. Years later, Hobbes' pupil was restored to the throne as Charles II, and the old teacher won a handsome pension.

Turn now to a very different scholar, Georg Wilhelm Friedrich Hegel (1770-1831), whose ideas were so controversial that other philosophers have been arguing about him ever since. He had the German passion for order, and his quest was to put everything in its place and so discover a unified system to explain the universe. He was famous equally for his dedication to work and for his convoluted ideas. At the University of Berlin he proved an awkward lecturer, but his students must have loved him. When he died suddenly of cholera, they sal-

163

vaged his notes and published some of his work posthumously.

Hegel held a hopeful view of the world, looking upon it as dynamic, constantly progressing and fulfilling. But to get to this concept he started with pessimism, then moved on to a theory of conflict before arriving at optimism. To put his theory into practice, he devised his famous formula: thesis plus antithesis equals synthesis.

Take any two opposites, Hegel said—for instance, the individual and the community. Call the individual the thesis. That makes the community the antithesis. Immediately conflict begins. How many rights should the individual possess? How many for the community? How can justice reconcile these conflicting needs? The clash can be fierce, but don't worry, said Hegel. That's what life, everything, everywhere, is all about. Thesis automatically generates its opposite, antithesis, and the fight is on. The negative is as vital as the positive to work things out. And they will work out. The two sides will battle, but the struggle will be resolved. And when it is, we will have synthesis. This won't just be one side emerging as the winner. The synthesis will be a product of both, and it will be more. It will come forth as something unique to itself, something brand new.

Why? How can we be sure the fighting will ever end? And if it does, how can we know something good will come of it? Because, said Hegel, the greatest opposites of all are the finite and infinite, and we know these have been resolved into one great synthesis.

Come again? How do we know any such thing? We know, said Hegel, because of the testimony of Chris-

164

tianity. Look at your Bible, look at the life of Christ. In God Himself we have infinity, the Absolute. That's the supreme example of thesis. Then God became man in Jesus. That's finite and it's antithesis. Jesus' life was struggle and suffering, culminating in the crucifixion. Then, moment of moments, all is transcended by the Resurrection. Humanity and the world are reconciled with God. That's the true synthesis.

After this, said Hegel, take any other pair of opposites there could ever be, and every one of them has to mirror this great divine playing out of thesis, antithesis and synthesis.

Hegel, no less than Hobbes, was a master of materialism and of realism, but in the end his logic led him straight to God. Who says philosophers can't be believers?

But how about Immanuel Kant?

The renowned German philosopher Immanuel Kant (1724-1804) surely has to be one of the most potent critics of religion ever. His studies in logic, held aloft as models for two centuries by his fellow scholars, systematically demolished the proofs for God advanced both by Anselm and Aquinas. If anybody ever shattered conventional ways of looking at the deity, it was Kant. He must have been an unbeliever, right?

In fact, he did believe. But this fact is sometimes overlooked even by students of Kant. To understand the thinking of this extraordinary man, we must remember the overwhelming clout his ideas have had on his fellow philosophers. Kant was among the first to treat the discipline of philosophy so methodically, so rigorously that it came to be something like a precise science. Since his lifetime every other philosopher has had to be counted either as a Kantian or an anti-Kantian. Germans for generations considered him the greatest of geniuses; elsewhere students may not have worshiped, but all have marveled.

Kant abounded in paradoxes. Both admirers and critics think of him as a giant, the "Thunderer" whose views must be respected, perhaps feared. Yet he was the mildest of men, barely five feet tall, in frail health yet managing to live eighty years, all of them in one town, Konigsberg.

Kant taught all his mature years at the University of Konigsberg. He never married. No monk ever lived a more regulated life. The townsfolk used to set their clocks by him. He rose at five every morning and lectured and worked at his desk by strict schedule. Every afternoon he took the same walk in all kinds of weather, sometimes causing his devoted servant, Lampe, to rush after him with an umbrella.

Over the years Kant poured out his thoughts in volume after volume, sometimes tightly written but sometimes – another paradox – so verbose and obscure that even experts differ about what he was trying to say. He made long strides in epistemology, the science of how people think, dismissing both the theory of John Locke that the mind is a *tabula rasa*, a blank slate that depends on impressions, and the ultimate skepticism of David Hume, who refused to assume that matter or even our minds exist. The truth lies between these views, Kant decided. Each of us has a mind and must use it to synthesize all sensations received from outside. But to do this – and here Kant pioneered new territory – the mind must have within it certain *a priori* concepts that we know instinctively are true.

Like what? Like the most basic facts we can conceive. Like truths that are absolute and necessary, that are "clear and certain in themselves." Like the obvious in mathematics, that "7 + 5 = 12," that the axioms of geometry are immutable, that the laws of space and time, science and nature go on forever and nothing can ever violate them. Our minds, said Kant, take this innate, built-in knowledge, mix it with the new data that experience is constantly pouring in, and analyze all of it. Thus we become thinking beings.

167

Now Kant turned his attention to God. Step by logical step he sought to destroy the carefully constructed theories that earlier philosophers had used to prove the existence of God. These don't work, Kant declared. We can't prove God by reason.

But Kant, contrary to the conclusions of some students with superficial knowledge, did not demolish God. We must go back to Kant's great idea that inside every human head there lurk those inborn, natural notions that precede reason, precede even our earliest infant perceptions. Among these, Kant believed, are the laws of morality. And these primitive concepts, more urges even than thoughts, happen to be much like the moral rules of Christianity. Each of us, Kant said, knows that we should be good, and we know it not by reason, not by experience, not by working out a cooperative way of life; rather, we know because the knowledge of good and evil has been placed in us from the very beginning. We know we ought to be good not just because we have learned this will make others be good to us but because in the deepest, most real sense we feel it is the right, the decent, thing to do.

Where do these bedrock, primal promptings come from? Did God plant them in our minds? In the end, can the reality of God be proved by the morality of human beings?

Kant made it clear that free will and the moral knowledge ingrained in each of us can only have been put there by a power outside ourselves. The intellect alone, Kant held, can never marshal enough evidence to confirm God's existence. But he came to believe that

168

moral proof does work. He put it this way: "I must not even say, '*It is* morally certain that there is a God' . . . but '*I am* morally certain.'"

So Immanuel Kant groped in his own way to faith. One of the mightiest, most exacting minds of all time arrived at the simple truth that belief can indeed transcend the force of logic. Even as he piled insight on insight, discovery on discovery, to build the splendid tower of his systematic philosophy, he stopped to consult his feelings, and there he found God.

Why do philosophers make such a big deal about God and "being"?

Philosophers and theologians love to talk about God in connection with "being." In fact, there is a whole branch of philosophy devoted to the study of being, called ontology. The word "being" itself became particularly popular in the 1930s when the German-born theologian Paul Tillich started teaching in the United States and worked out his famous definition of God as the "Ground of All Being."

Certainly if one believes in God, it is proper to think of Him as the Ground of All Being. But does Tillich's concept, which has since been refined by many others, really go far enough? Isn't there a personal dimension to God?

We had better start by making sure we know what "being" in this context means. Seven hundred years before Tillich, Thomas Aquinas had his own ideas about God and being. Everything has being or it doesn't, Thomas thought. Either it exists or it doesn't exist. Then Thomas reasoned that there is a sense in which something can exist more than something else, can in a sense have a more developed being. This involves potential. Everything that exists, you, me, the guy next door, this rock, that clump of earth, exists right now but also has existed in the past and will exist in the future. And in its past and in its future it has been and will be at least slightly different. That's because everything changes. Obviously we change, but so does everything else, even the rock and clod of earth. They change their positions because the Earth keeps turning and they change their shapes because erosion keeps acting on them.

This constant process of change means everything has a potential. It is going to be something different either sooner or later. It is going to keep trying to fulfill its own potential. But will it? Not according to Thomas' theory. The great cycle of existence spins on. You and I are going to become dust and ashes, fossils and gas. The atoms whirling in us will change when they whirl in something else. The most microscopic elements we know will keep changing, and so will the giant galaxies spinning in the heavens.

But one thing will not change in this way. That is God. It seems almost irreverent, but God has no potential. All the rest of us do. The big difference is that God alone is perfectly fulfilled. Right now He is everything He needs to be. He is perfect being.

All this proves the difficulty of describing the divine in limited human terms. So in the never-ending quest for truth, thinkers today are going beyond Aquinas, beyond Tillich's definition. They are even wondering if God can be beyond being. For instance, Jean-Luc Marion, professor of philosophy at the University of Paris, argues in *God Without Being* (University of Chicago Press, 1991) that God is indeed free from all categories of being. This, Marion assures us, does not mean God does not exist. "At issue here," he explains, "is not the possibility of God's attaining Being, but, quite the opposite, the possibility of Being's attaining God."

According to Marion, the concept of being is not big enough to disclose the reality of God. In a way, the fact of being even imprisons God. Marion believes that God's "liberation from Being" means that God "comes to us in and as a gift." God's great gift of love to us stands prior to and beyond all being.

The American theologian Father David Tracy agrees that God cannot be thought of as "somehow constricted by Being." This, says Tracy, would mean that God is "somehow less than God."

I wonder what Thomas Aquinas would think of such advanced notions. My guess is he would say that to posit a God without being simply begs the question of Who God is. Thomas' great idea was that God not only exists and has being but also exists in a way nothing else exists. Thomas would insist that to say that only God has perfect being really means something. For instance, an object cannot be perfectly white because it is not in itself "whiteness," that is it is not the essence of "whiteness." God, and only God, both exists and is the essence of existence. Put it another way: God not only *has* goodness, power, love, perfection; He *is* goodness, power, love, perfection.

I find Thomas' positive concepts more comforting than the negative ones that deny God has being. Thomas builds an image in my mind that I can't erase. Here am I and everything else in the universe existing way down on one plane, being and changing, striving for but never reaching a potential. And then there's God, way up there on another plane, off in the mists of mystery, beyond space and time, creating us, loving us, blessedly existing, infinitely being, gloriously fulfilled.

Yet the curious fact is that my putting God way up there on that distant, lonely plane of a completely different way of being doesn't in the least make Him seem more remote and far away. Somehow I feel more certain than ever that God is some place else, too. He is right here, right now, with me.

What's all this about "existentialism"?

Existentialism is tough to understand and everybody seems to have a different definition for it. Most dictionaries would agree that existentialism is a system of thought that centers on the individual and the individual's relationship to the universe and to God. After that, take your pick.

Philosophers, each doing their own thing and as always pretty sure of themselves, love to contrast existentialism with what they call essentialism. By this they mean that if you believe in existentialism you believe that concrete, individual existence is more important than (in philosopher's jargon this is usually stated as "precedes") the basic essence or the permanent underlying reality of a thing. Backers of essentialism believe just the opposite.

Of course, definitions and theories like these don't get far in the real world, so while the philosophers keep complicating the problem, the rest of us have to try to simplify it. If you hang onto that concept of individual existence being more important than anything else, you can move quickly to another idea that gets close to the core of existentialism. This is that each human being is free and has the innate ability to make choices. This in turn means that because humans can choose, we are more than mere playthings of history and of nature's whims. We make choices and we are responsible for our actions.

Unhappily, some philosophers see a gloomy side to this. They hold that this very freedom to choose brings about those feelings of dread and anguish we all endure part of the time. So existentialism is bad, right?

Not really. A way to understand is to go back to the man who started it all. Soren Kierkegaard is the father of existentialism. He burned out in a hurry, living only from 1813 to 1855, and nobody outside his native Denmark paid much attention to his views for nearly a hundred years. Then, almost overnight, he became a cult figure. To understand Kierkegaard, you have to understand his life, and a lonely, almost desperate life it was.

Soren came from a well-to-do family and was able to live without working in Copenhagen. He became engaged to a 17-year-old beauty, Regina Olsen, then decided he wasn't good enough for her. She eventually married a man who became governor of the Danish West Indies, and Soren stayed unhappily in love with her for the rest of his life. He was frail and melancholy, and the adjective all his contemporaries agree upon is "lonely." Before he died at age 42 he poured out his philosophy in volume after volume of hastily written and often bitter diaries and books.

Kierkegaard's guiding idea was that conventional philosophers, sitting in their comfortable studies, cannot work out the problems of existence. Humans, he insisted, cannot learn objectively but only subjectively. We can learn not as spectators but only through personal, passionate experience.

What can we learn? We can learn, said Kierkegaard, about God. But the way is not easy. God is not some par-

175

adoxical presence inside humans. God is separated from us by estrangement, and there is only one way – a very difficult way – to reach God.

Each person, Kierkegaard believed, is a lonely soul in a lonely universe. We will never know enough to come to faith in God through the intellect. Moreover, we cannot achieve faith from anything we learn from anybody else. There is only one way to achieve faith and that is by a venture of the will. We can know God only by confronting Him. We have to reveal ourselves to God, give Him our total trust. To know God we must realize our infinite distance from Him. And the only way to overcome this distance is a very daring way indeed. We must make a leap of faith.

That is the heart of Kierkegaard's philosophy – a leap of faith. If we can make that leap, we can do anything. Without it we have nothing. Each of us must decide to dare or not to dare.

It's this idea that gave birth to existentialism. Of course, plenty of other minds have worked on the concept and changed it. But for Christian existentialists the center has held firm. Faith is not a matter of understanding because human beings will never be able to understand God. Nor is faith a matter of taking authority from the Bible or the church. Rather, faith, first and last, is a product of the will. Each of us, lonely and alone, must summon our own private courage and seize the initiative to confront God. Personal existence, experience, gives us more knowledge than any authority or any abstract system ever could.

Of course, some later secular existentialists have found danger in the daring premise that we really possess full freedom and responsibility. Perhaps the most famous was Jean-Paul Sartre (1905-1980). He, too, led a hard life, fighting with the French resistance, then being held as a prisoner during World War II. In novels, plays and essays, he propounded the sad side of existentialism, Yes, we must choose, agreed Sartre, but we must do so not because there is a God but because there is no God. What's more, there is no real standard of ethics. We are all, concluded Sartre, condemned to live in the dark.

Sartre's despair echoes Kierkegaard's loneliness. But Kierkegaard found a way out. He made that brave leap of faith. He found God.

You and I also have a choice whether or not to dare to leap. I think I have made Kierkegaard's leap, and I'm glad.

How about that weird "process theology"?

Why do we have to make things so complicated? Why can't we just have a "simple" belief in God? That's a good question many Christians ask, and for good reason. But there are times when "simple" doesn't get us far enough. If you've never wondered about that relatively new concept called "process theology," you could skip this section. But if you're willing to try one more way of looking at God, it might be worth a try.

Alfred North Whitehead (1861-1947) is the father of process theology. Basically, this admittedly difficult philosophy asserts that reality does not consist of substances and beings with stable natures but rather is made up of endless chains of occasions of becoming. These occasions, sometimes termed "energy events," occur in the blink of an eye and are strung together in continuous sequences like the frames of a movie. Each of these super-fast happenings is directed by what Whitehead calls a "subjective aim." This aim is forever reaching restlessly into the future, trying to realize its full potential and achieve its real self. Under this concept, the idea of being slips into relative insignificance. What's vital is the idea of becoming.

If I understand Whitehead and his followers properly, this notion of the all-important becoming holds true not only for animate beings like us but also for inanimate matter. It runs through all of creation and goes so far as to allow a hint of self-determination for such tiny, basic building blocks as atoms and electrons. The theory even holds true for God. Thus God fits right into the ongoing reality we perceive and acts constantly through time throughout the universe. In fact, some proponents of process theology maintain that it is God Who supplies those "subjective aims" that drive everybody and everything down the road to becoming.

The theorists go further. They contend that in the great push and pull of Process (process theologians like to capitalize their favorite word), God Himself is acted upon and is actually changed. He reacts to events; for instance, He adapts to the decisions of the creatures to whom He has given free will.

If we believe this theory, we have to make a shift in our usual way of looking at God. If we say that God is affected by events, are we not limiting His omnipotence? So be it, say some process theologians. They are willing to picture a finite God. They see God as sharing power with those whom He has empowered to make free decisions.

All pretty complicated. But it seems to me that no matter how far the Process folk wander from conventional beliefs, their basic tenet is sound. When all is said and done, the heart of process theology appears to come back to a simple but overwhelming fact we "simpler" Christians have believed for 2,000 years: Unlike the Process proponents, we do believe God to be omnipotent. But, like them, we also know God to be ongoing, active, vital. How do we know? Because we can feel God, now and always, acting within us and guarding and guiding us as His Holy Spirit. What's more, we believe that if God reacts this very day to our prayers, that in no way diminishes Him. He acts — and if necessary, reacts to us — because He loves us. That, we "simple" Christians believe, makes God greater than ever.

Is there a "theology of hope"?

One of the happier Christian beliefs is that there can be such a thing as a "theology of hope." This isn't altogether wishful thinking. After all, the core of the New Testament is the Good News of Christ. That surely means a Christian has reason to look to the future with optimism. The trouble is that everybody who tries to develop a full-blown theology of hope seems to have a different idea, so I guess I'm entitled to my view, too.

Many of those who believe in the hope theory tie it to the premise that throughout history things have been gradually getting better and that the trend will continue. They think human beings have been perfecting themselves, have been steadily coming of age, and in time to come can expect to live ever richer, fuller and freer lives. Depending on whom you listen to, God can play a big part in this scenario or humans can star pretty much by themselves.

A truly Christian theology of hope, of course, puts God right at the center: We can achieve nothing without God's help. But I think a Christian has to go further than that. For a Christian, the coming of Jesus, the Incarnation and the Resurrection, the Good News all add up to a hope already achieved. For us hope is here. It has been right along. Jesus came to us and is with us still.

So what can a Christian hope for that we don't already have? Will the human condition get better or might things grow worse? Well, there are plenty of doomsayers around. If you want a terrifying look at the future, you need only read such creative works as H. G.

181

Wells' *The Time Machine*, Aldous Huxley's *Brave New World* or George Orwell's *Nineteen Eighty-Four*. Each of these observant writers – and there are plenty of others – brings to vivid life a particularly chilling view of what may lie ahead. They succeed because they have the perception to pick out individual threads in modern civilization that could lead to disaster.

But for a Christian, there can be other answers. As for me, I cherish my own private little theology of hope for the future of mankind. Follow me as I divide the whole of human history into four ages:

The first age could be the Age of Survival, when we humans were guided by the instinct just to live, to hunt and to gather. In those primitive times, either by ourselves or with the tribe, we exhausted our energies scrabbling for the essentials of life.

The second age could be the one we're in now. Call it the Age of Profit, but a less kind name would be the Age of Greed. Possessions own us; self-interest guides us. The goal of each of us is to take care of number one, to set aside all we can for ourselves and our particular loved ones and yield only as much as we are forced to give to the commonweal.

The third age is hard to imagine, and we could even call it the Age of Benevolence. This will come when we know we should be good to our fellow humans because it is the right thing to do. We learn to make enough sacrifices so nobody suffers. We race through life not to grasp and to win but to help and to share.

The fourth age is even harder to see through the mists of time. Here at last, in a future so dim we hardly dare to glimpse it, we come to the Age of Love. At last we fully feel our love for God and His love for us. We love Him so well, in fact, that we love all our fellow humans, too. And, wonder of wonders, we find that the giving – and the living – is a joy. In this truly new world it will be easy to see God; we will just look at each other.

Ah well, all this is only my private dream. Perhaps Wells and Huxley and Orwell and the other futurists are right. Perhaps we are doomed to selfishness and unhappiness. Yet that is not the Christian way. It is not what Jesus taught.

So I'll keep my dream. If I dream hard enough, who knows, it might come true.

Why did God bother to create?

It's a question that fascinates some philosophers: Was it better for God to have created or not to have created? It's also a question that many of us would place pretty high on the ho-hum list. We can't know the answer, so who cares?

Yet if as Christians, our duty is to use the minds God gave us to get to know Him as well as our intellects will allow, perhaps we should probe even such an imponderable as this. Put the question this way: God can do anything. He had a choice. He started with chaos, a mass of nothing. But out of this nothing, *ex nihilo*, He chose to create us and everything else. Why?

First of all, we have to realize that anything we can consider has to be, like a poll, a mere sampling – and a very small one at that. We can only look at a tiny bit of God's creation – our universe – and we can't see much of that. There is, of course, the possibility that in other galaxies there may be other beings far holier or far more sinful than we, other environments far more comfortable or far more brutal than ours. Then, too, there are those other "worlds" way below or way above us, so microscopic we can't see them or so huge that we are microscopic to them. So our sample can be only a vertical slice – leaving out the other galaxies – and only a horizontal slice – limited to worlds roughly our size.

But we have to make do with what we have. Looking at our planet, is it better for God to have created the life we see all around us? How about the short, driven, cruel life in the animal kingdom, where each creature spends its time desperately as predator trying to assuage hunger or as hunted trying to escape capture? Perhaps we know so little about the minds and feelings of these creatures that we can't even guess whether their lives are worth it. So we must turn to the animal we know best, and perhaps even here we can know our fellow human beings so imperfectly that we must narrow the sample even further. Each of us may have to seek the answer only within our own individual heads.

Was it better that God created me? On a fine spring day, in good health, loved and loving, my answer, of course, is yes. But what if I were in pain, hungry, cold, afraid, without hope?

At this point, I think, we have to remember that we have not only left out the "horizontal" and "vertical" worlds, we have left out heaven and hell. Hell is separation from God and we know we should try to avoid it. But as Christians, we believe that a heaven must be there, and if it is, it supplies part of the answer.

If creation – this life – is a doorway to heaven, then it is better, surely, that we were created. Humans, I believe, have good reason to be grateful for the gift of creation. Even when we are desperate, there lies in us the feeling that there is indeed Somewhere else that we are reaching for, that beckons, that lies beyond the here and now. We feel, we know, that there is not only Something else but Someone else. We know that God cares for us, and that He will take us to a better place no matter what the pain now. Christians know deep down that God means for us to be happy.

So that is part of the answer why I am glad God created me. Another part is that I have, right now, God's great gift of life. With this I have the gift of my loved ones. And I have, above all, the immeasurable gift of God's love. This gift does not need to wait for heaven. It is here. Could it even be that God created all of creation because He loves me?

How can grown-ups believe in angels?

The idea of angels goes back way before Christianity. The word *angel* comes from both Hebrew and Greek for "messenger." Tradition has it that these creatures, lower than God but higher than humans, fly on swift wings between heaven and earth. Their mission is to save us from harm, to comfort us, or to bring us extraordinary tidings. Angels often radiate light. Some people tell of seeing them; others only hear them or feel their presence. They have figured in religions from the ancient Persians and Egyptians to American Indians to modern Buddhism and Hinduism. The Koran invokes angels frequently; the Bible mentions them some 300 times.

In the Old Testament, angels not only brought messages to Abraham and Moses and others, but also showed such vigor that one wrestled Jacob all night while another single-handedly slew 185,000 Assyrians. In the New Testament, angels are gentler. Gabriel prepared Mary for glory; heralds sang for joy at Bethlehem; angels fortified Jesus in the wilderness; one comforted Him at Gethsemane, and another rolled the stone from the tomb.

Early Christians never doubted the reality of angels. Everybody was thought to possess his or her guardian angel. Then the picture grew darker. If you had a good angel, why not an evil one, too? You could have a good and a bad one perched on each shoulder. This heaped fuel on the debates over temptation, sin and salvation that ultimately had to be thrashed out at the great creedal councils.

In the 6th century, a scholarly mystic whose real name we don't know but who wrote as Dionysius the Areopagite scoured Scripture and the early church fathers to array all angels neatly into three categories or "choirs," each with three subdivisions. The highest, the seraphim, cherubim and thrones, were celestial courtiers who gathered around God in heaven and were so holy a mortal would die if he or she ever glimpsed one. Next came the dominions, powers and authorities, whose might spread to the physical universe. Last came the beings sent to earth, the principalities, archangels and angels.

In the 13th century, Thomas Aquinas made such an exhaustive study of angels that we know him as the Angelic Doctor. He surveyed the great chain of being that stretches from the inanimate up to the divine, then concluded that without angels as a link, "the universe would be incomplete." Other thinkers contested his findings, and the debate wore on for centuries, eventually provoking such put-down arguments as how many angels can stand on the head of a pin. Meanwhile, simpler folk ignored the learned bickering; they took Scripture – and angels — literally. Moreover, if you had seen an angel, and many insisted they had, you believed.

Angels flourished in the imagination, most of all in art. Wings grew bigger, halos brighter. The very word "angel" seemed to trip from the tongues of poets. Shakespeare had Horatio bid Hamlet, "Good night, sweet prince, and flights of angels sing thee to thy rest."

Keats spoke of an "angel's tear that falls through the clear ether silently." Longfellow sang of "the lovely stars, the forget-me-nots of the angels." Lincoln besought North and South to unite through "the better angels of our nature."

In time angels began to be seen not only as God's messengers but also as spirits dwelling within us. By the Age of Enlightenment they had shifted from religious and awesome to secular and sentimental.

But the spiritual need for angels never died. Our own era is seeing an angelic explosion. Reports of encounters with angels fill periodicals and the airwaves. Scriptwriters rely on them for plots. Discussion groups and seminars abound. Angel-watchers swap sightings on the Internet. We hear of angel power and we can study angelology.

Is it a fad, part of the modern fascination with the occult? Is it wish projection, a yearning for a bit of heaven here on earth? Or will it prove to be a meaningful, even a lasting, development in our search to understand God?

There is reason for hope. Through the long sweep of history angels have bolstered our faith. Aquinas had a point with his missing link. Ever since we began to look humbly up to the unbearably bright glory of God, we have found the need for an intermediary. Angels have helped us bridge the gap.

God is so far beyond our imaginative powers that we need ways to dramatize Him, make Him personal, create images. Angels channel our thoughts and guide

189

us to God. They help us pray. They fasten our souls to God.

Perhaps the German Dominican Johannes Eckhart, back in the 14th century, came as close to the truth as anybody. If we seek God, he said, we must look into our souls and there a "spark" will ignite. This could be the work of an angel because, explained Meister Eckhart, "That's all an angel is, an idea of God."

Does Jesus love some people more than others?

True or false? "Jesus liked some people more than others." That question was posed to a church study group some years ago. I had marked the statement false and was surprised to find many others considered it true. Arguments were brought out that Jesus had a particular liking or love for His beloved Apostle John and for Lazarus and Mary and Martha and that He much preferred the company of the poor and lowly to the rich and mighty.

All true, but I contended that Jesus had perfect, infinite love for every human being – then, now and always – and that this overpowering love swept away any silly little likes and dislikes. I don't know if I convinced anyone, but today I am more certain than ever that Jesus' love is truly infinite and that it must have been so even during the time He spent among us. And because His love is infinite, He must have loved everyone equally. He must have loved even the money changers He chased from the Temple. We can dare to believe that He even loved the Roman soldiers as they drove the nails into His wrists and feet.

The love Jesus felt while He walked the Earth perfectly reflects God's love. How can such love not be distributed equally to all? God starts us all off on the same footing through life. He gives us free will and hopes that each of us eventually will turn freely to Him.

"God does not play dice," Albert Einstein once declared. He was protesting against the uncertainty principle proposed by his colleagues to explain the quirky antics of quantum physics, but I think there is a completely different sense in which God really does gamble. He gambles on each of us. He created us and He loves us, but He lets us find our own way. He loves us like loving parents who watch their child ride a bike or go off to school for the first time. The parents want to protect forever, but they know that for the sake of the child there comes a time when they must let go.

God lets us go, too. He hopes we'll come back to Him, but it's a gamble. He is watching and He loves every one of us equally – sinners and saints and the whole world in between.

Why does it help to keep the seasons of the church year?

Christian worship revolves around the life of Christ. Christ, in fact, is the pivot on which the seasons of the church year turn. Does it have to be this way? Perhaps not, but since the dawn of Christianity, believers have merged their adoration of the Lord as tightly as possible into the cycle of their daily lives.

It makes sense. If we are to pray to Jesus, to praise Him, to thank Him and, above all, to ask Him for things, we have to hold Him in our minds. We have to feel His presence and to remember what we have been told and what we have learned about Him. One way to keep the memory fresh is to try to relive His life. We can do so, to be sure, only in a tiny and limited human fashion. But we can try to celebrate the events of His time on earth, in a roughly chronological order, and to think about them on the appointed days and seasons. Thus, Christians commemorate Jesus' birth, death, resurrection, ascension and a number of happenings in between.

Of course, we can't be too literal about this. For starters, we don't really know enough about Jesus' life. Even when we try to celebrate the period we have the best record for, the time of Jesus' active ministry, we run into problems. The three synoptic Gospels, Matthew, Mark and Luke, recount this period as a single year; John makes it three years. So we have to do the best we can. No modern scholar, for instance, believes Jesus was actually born on December 25 or that He was crucified on a particular Friday in the spring. The dates are arrived at only because they conform best to the records of Jewish festivals and other historical clues.

So the holy days Christians celebrate serve basically as reminders. We go to church or pray at home thinking about Jesus and remembering a particular aspect of Him. The object is to bring us closer to Him, and I, for one, find it works.

Do we have to be sad during Lent?

Lent is the holiest season of the Christian year. It leads up to the saddest day of the year, Good Friday, and to the greatest and happiest day of all, Easter Sunday. Lent starts on Ash Wednesday and lasts 40 days, not counting Sundays. Christians use it as a time to remember and to think. Many find it helps to make a sacrifice by performing a special good deed or giving up a particular comfort. In any case, it is a time to concentrate on that enormous sacrifice Jesus made for our sakes. It is even a time to try to relive – again in a merely human and hopelessly inadequate way – the agony He endured.

How can we even begin to relive the agony of Christ? How could I, even for a moment, imagine, much less enter into, the loneliness and dread Jesus felt in the Garden of Gethsemane, the shame He endured before the Sanhedrin and Pontius Pilate, the torture He bore at the hands of the Roman soldiers, the hideous pain of the nails tearing into His flesh, the horror of the slow strangling and sagging and bleeding to death on the Cross?

Does God really want me to feel all this? I don't believe it, but I think there is something God very much wants me to do. And Lent is a perfect time to do it. This is to remember my sins. If I really think hard about them, actually cringe at the thought of them, I, too, am suffering. It is, of course, only the smallest, remotest fraction of what Jesus suffered for us, but it just might be enough to bring me closer to Him. For if I think hard enough about my sins, try to reconstruct them as best I can, recall my wrongs of omission as well as commission, really relive them, sincerely seek forgiveness, then I am not only getting closer to Jesus but I may be doing something else. I may find myself vowing to do better. I may promise myself – and Jesus – that I will try to live a better life. I may promise Him that I will try to be worthy of His love.

That perhaps is what Lent should be all about – a time to remember Jesus, to remember His suffering and to make ourselves suffer just a little bit. It is not a time for masochism; it is a time to try to make ourselves better. Jesus can help us.

Christians have found that if they bring themselves to make a real effort during Lent, if they try to become better people, if they try to think of Jesus' agony especially on Good Friday, then a moment of true happiness can await them. They find that after this time of prayer and preparation, the sun can rise with true glory and true joy on Easter Sunday morning.

How can wafers and wine be Jesus' body and blood?

At the very heart of worship in most main-line branches of Christianity lies that service known as the Eucharist or the Holy Communion or the Mass. It is here, many Christians believe, that they realize most fully the presence of Jesus. The ceremony is based on the commands Jesus gave the Apostles at the Last Supper. Worshipers physically partake of perfectly ordinary bread and wine that is considered by God's grace to have been transformed into the body and blood of Christ.

How can anybody actually believe such an extraordinary transformation? We live in an era of science, a time of sophisticated chemical analysis. Perhaps this very physical method of worship served a purpose in the early days, but can it have meaning now?

Most Christians would answer yes. But if we ask how literally we are to consider the actual change of elements, we will get a range of answers. Some believe the ritual is a holy and fitting commemoration of the way Jesus asked us to remember Him at the Last Supper. They believe we can reverently eat the bread and taste the wine without actually believing that a physical change has taken place. Other traditions of Christianity hold firmly that the wafers and wine genuinely are, actually and physically, the "real presence" of Jesus. These Christians believe that we are consuming His body and so in a mystical fashion are becoming a part of Him and He of us.

Thomas Aquinas was a strong proponent of the latter view. He reached back fifteen centuries to pagan times to the great Greek philosopher Aristotle (384-322 B. C.) to explain this mysterious process of transubstantiation. Aristotle had made a distinction between what he called "substance" as "that which exists and is not in another thing" and what he called "accident" as "that which is other than the essence," such as size or shape or taste. All the changes we know about are changes of accident, as when water becomes ice, wool becomes a sweater, a baby becomes a man.

Now Thomas Aquinas reasoned that the miracle of the Eucharist must involve a change of a more profound kind. This one-and-only transformation far transcends our knowledge of change and must include a factor that makes it different from all other changes. He concluded that in the unique change that takes place in the Eucharist – and in this change only – the facts of the change are precisely reversed. In normal changes the accidents change and the substance does not, but in the Eucharist the accidents do not change and the substance does. Thus the bread and wine remain the same to human eyes, but their real substance is transformed into Christ's body and blood. What we see and taste are bread and wine; what is really there is Jesus Himself.

Other minds of old have brought other theories to the Eucharist. Thomas a Kempis in the 15th century came up with the thought that when we come into church the light of Jesus would be so bright that we "could not bear to behold" Him. So, Thomas believed, our Lord thoughtfully hid Himself "under this Holy

Sacrament," and we can all find Him there if we look properly.

How literally to take the change of bread and wine into Jesus' body and blood will probably remain a source of difference as long as Christianity endures. Perhaps the best answer is to pay less attention to analyzing the degree of reality of the "real presence" and instead devote ourselves more fully to the service itself. The fact is that over the centuries countless believers have found enormous comfort, renewal and hope by kneeling and praying and confessing at the altar of the Eucharist and then physically partaking of the Sacrament. For many no moment could ever be more holy. No moment could touch their hearts as much or make them sense a closer communion with Jesus. It is not a matter of thinking but of feeling.

For the Eucharist to be felt, each participant must play a part. We in the congregation can't just sit in the pew and wait to receive. We must offer to God not only the gifts of wafers and wine that go up to the altar to be consecrated, but we must offer to Him our very selves. The core of the service is a prayer that asks God please to take this bread and this wine and make them become *for us* the body and blood of Christ. We have to ask for it to happen, we have to pray hard and earnestly that this holy mystery will indeed mean something for us. Only then can we begin to feel the reality. And millions have found that there is reality provided we ask enough and want enough. In his poem *Christmas* John Betjeman has testified to this: "Nor all the steeple-shaking bells/ Can with this single Truth compare—/ That God was Man in

Palestine/ And lives to-day in Bread and Wine" (*Collected Poems*, Houghton Mifflin Co., 1958).

So the Eucharist is far more than a pious metaphor. It can be for each of us as much of a miracle as we are willing to let it be. First, we have to prepare for the service by remembering our sins, asking God's forgiveness and vowing to do better. Then we have to approach the altar wanting to come just as close to Jesus as we can. If we truly and honestly yearn to receive His Blessed Sacrament, we can be sure He will give it to us.

We must leave our doubts aside. C. S. Lewis once wrote: "The command, after all, was Take, eat: not Take, understand."

Is there a "natural law"?

The term "natural law" is being bandied about a good deal these days, and there seems to be confusion about what it means. It's a prime example of twisting words Alice-in-Wonderland-style to let them mean anything we want. Since everybody else is doing it, I may as well set forth my own definition.

Some people hold natural law to be that code of ethics that humans arrive at by reason. I think this is a wrong, even a contradictory, use of the term.

Some say natural law is that pattern of behavior made known to us by divine Revelation. I think this also is inaccurate.

A third definition of natural law is that it is a system of morality that is ingrained into our minds from the very start of our lives, that it is known to us even before reason can begin, even before we can learn by Revelation through such channels as praying or reading the Bible. I think this is the most precise and useful meaning of the term natural law.

To be sure, these three meanings overlap to some extent. But there is a long history for that third meaning, for the belief that a code of ethics common to everyone – Christian, Buddhist, atheist, what have you – exists and that it has been implanted in the human psyche since the beginning of mankind. Plato and Aristotle both endorsed the idea, at least partially. Thomas Aquinas was sure of it. As we have seen, no less a philosopher than Immanuel Kant used a natural law ingrained into the human mind as a basis for his personal belief in

God. C. S. Lewis, wrote a book, *The Abolition of Man* (Macmillan, 1947), to argue the theory. Moreover, Lewis included a detailed appendix to show that religions from the beginning of recorded history have all held the same basic laws of morality. In 1993 Pope John Paul II issued an encyclical on morality, *Veritatis splendor* (The Splendor of Truth), using a pre-ordained natural law as its premise.

Sorry, but I can't buy the theory. I don't believe that there is a moral code implanted in us like some supernatural bit of DNA. There is just no reason to suppose so. Here we have to apply Occam's razor. We have no need to reach for a complex, far-out explanation when a simpler one is close at hand. The more obvious explanation is that human beings have arrived at a common moral code through pure reason. Do good unto others and good will be done unto you. That's the essence of humanity's ethical code all the way back to the tribal cooperation of the cavemen, on to the Ten Commandments of Moses, to the Golden Rule of Jesus, to modern laws of behavior that embrace everything from obeying decisions of the U. S. Supreme Court to waiting in line at the supermarket.

All these rules are based on logic and have proved useful for people trying to rub along with each other in the business of life. I see no need to posit that the knowledge for such conduct was placed into our minds in some metaphysical fashion. All the rules could have been reached by means of the reasoning power that God has given us.

My theory is that God endowed each of us with a brain and wants us to use it. He so made the world that we have to grope and grapple. We must use our minds to work out the dilemmas of life and to face the challenges of getting along with our fellow humans. To do so we have to keep sifting and resifting the rights and wrongs. The world doesn't hold still. Times and circumstances change. Rules can't be written in stone.

We must always pray to God for guidance. Each of us must listen to Him through our own conscience. We must ever beware of letting the ends justify the means. We must not only teach our children the basics of morality but we must show them by example. We must be flexible enough to keep using our brains and to bring as good judgment as we can to every new predicament. The struggle to be good is much more complicated and much more difficult than simply consulting a list of laws. Hard as it may prove, we can never duck the task of applying the arduous and always slippery ideals of situational ethics.

Along the way something important happens. As we use this brain of ours to live in the world, we listen to and understand God's Revelation. While we work through the problems of survival, while we study and while we pray, we come to know God and Jesus and the Holy Spirit. If we use our minds – and open our hearts – we discover what Revelation points to. It points to love. We learn to love God and to know that He loves us.

Once we have mastered that, the rest is easy. Then we know that love rules all. We love God so much that we can love our fellow human beings, and ethics and morals and good conduct follow as the night the day. We live by law, but, more important, we live by love.

Aren't believers afraid of "playing God"?

"You can't play God!" is a familiar shout these days.

But the fact is we're going to have to try.

The time for decisions about genetic engineering is upon us. DNA researchers have the means to start tinkering with human heredity in a big way. Their scalpels are poised, their petri dishes ready, and they're only waiting for the legislators and the moralists to say go. Scientists are cloning farm animals, and the know-how to tackle people can't be far off. Already we have the tools to produce a healthier human race. Now we have to decide whether and how to use them.

This whole field and others related to it pose desperately tangled problems, and one strand of the knot is bound to lead us to particularly wrenching choices. Doctors can spot deformities in a fetus long before birth. Should they allow it to be born? Should the law decide? Should the parents? If, guided by instinct and compassion, we agree to let the mother make this awful judgment, are we copping out? Will the birth of a physically or mentally incurable child doom it – and the parents – to lifetimes of despair and sacrifice? What's best for all concerned? How do we know what's really incurable? Who decides?

If we dare to delve into the genetic future of our progeny, will we know when and where to stop? Is even to venture into such uncharted waters too much for our ethical prowess? Are we now, can we ever be, wise enough to use science to chart our biological destinies?

The questions multiply as our technical know-how expands. We have appointed commissions and probably we'll name plenty more. But science is the hare and morality the tortoise. The deciders are dragging and the doers are ready. Wisdom and caution may lose by default.

History waves a warning flag. Take the Germans. At the start of the 20th century they stood among the most cultivated peoples of the earth. Their scholars were preeminent not only in many areas of technology but also in philosophy, in theology, in all the gentler arts that contemplate God and comfort our human condition. Then, suddenly, Gotterdammerung and dreams of conquest. Goosesteps trampled and gas ovens wiped out the civility of generations. Almost overnight Hitler convinced Germans that destiny and duty demanded they produce a master race.

Take ourselves. We disown AIDS victims and cage our poor in ghettoes. We men have just learned to treat women as equals, sort of. We're not nearly smart enough or good enough to disregard differences in human skin colors or ethnic backgrounds. Morally we're still in the playpen.

If we can't handle problems with such obvious solutions, how are we going to face the ethics of masterminding our genes? The trouble is we don't have time to mature. We need a dose of wisdom now.

If we are going to presume to play God, we had better go to Him for some pointers. We had better pray to Him and we had better listen.

We might be surprised. We might learn, for instance, that God doesn't oppose our trying to play His role. This doesn't mean He's going to stand aside and let us take over. It does mean He gave us brains and means for us to use them. He also gave us a conscience and the knowledge to tell good from evil.

God equipped us to tackle problems. He made the universe and the rules. He gave us His grace and all His love, and He is always here to guide us. But He doesn't tell us how to do everything. He wants us to make decisions. And with every choice we either do His will or we don't, we either turn a little bit of ourselves toward Him or away from Him. It is in fact exactly by this path of making tough decisions every day all through our lives that God wants us to make our way to Him.

Can we face with courage the dauntingly difficult ethical problems involved in cloning and all the other aspects of genetic engineering? Can we learn not only to make these decisions but also to make them with tolerance for the beliefs of others?

We can no longer ask whether we should make such judgments. We know now that we will have to.

Yes, we will have to play God. And the way to learn how is to get on our knees and look up at the Master.

Which is more important, faith or good works?

Volumes of scholarly thought and argument have poured forth on the divisive issue of faith versus good works. The debate is almost as old as Christendom, going back at least to the Epistles of Paul and of James. St. Paul, with an enthusiastic boost a millennium and a half later from Martin Luther, contended that good works count for nothing without faith. A person, Paul told the Galatians, "is not justified by works of the law but through faith in Jesus Christ" (2:16). On the other hand, the Epistle of James could hardly disagree more directly. A person, St. James declares unequivocally, "is justified by works and not by faith alone" (2:24).

I had always sided with Paul and his great theory of justification by faith. I believe, along with Luther and the reformers, that faith is the key to atonement with God. I believe we can and should be wholeheartedly thankful for the wondrous, unmerited gift of Jesus dying for our sins and also for all the blessings of this life. If we believe enough and so be thankful enough, good works will flow from us naturally. With enough faith and enough gratitude and enough sheer, joyful love for God, we can hardly fail to be good. In fact, we can hope to be so grateful and so happy to be loved by God that we may some day find ourselves good without even having to think about it.

So James, I thought, seemed to have the matter backward. His argument appeared to be that you should do good because it is right, and as a result God will reward you. This to me smacked too much of a bargain with God, a *quid pro quo*. I was convinced that James' reasoning fell short of my cherished, dearly held belief that love leads the way and that we can achieve atonement with God only through justification by faith.

But I've had to revise my early thinking. This came about from a rereading of the whole Epistle of James. To my dismay I found that I had been taking this great early Christian (possibly a brother of Jesus, no less!) out of context. Then I saw how both Paul and James could be correct. Basically they are reaching the same conclusion but coming at it from opposite directions.

Paul says that faith – he uses the word essentially in the sense of trust – produces love of God and gratitude and hence good works. But James doesn't really disagree. He, or whoever used his name to write this stirring epistle, is warning against a particular fallacy among the Christians of that day – and of our day, too. If you read the whole letter, you see that James is making it clear that some people give lip service to Jesus but ignore the needs of their fellow humans. Faith, or what they claim to be faith, is thus a sham. It's no good to believe intellectually in Jesus, James argues, if at the same time you are not willing to put your love and your service and your pocketbook where your mouth is.

Paul almost certainly never had a chance to read this moving letter of James, but I think the great Apostle to the Gentiles would have endorsed it. The two saints travel toward the truth by different paths, and the blessed result is that both manage to get there. We today might worry less about which is more important, faith or good works, and try harder to practice both.

How can I be good if I feel like sinning?

In our day emotions are kings. From cradle to grave we are urged by everybody from kindergarten teachers to psychiatrists to old-age counselors to let it all hang out. Don't hold it in, they tell us. Let your feelings show.

Good advice, of course. Mental health depends on allowing our sentiments to flow freely from us instead of clotting up inside our psyche. Analysts have achieved remarkable results by probing back and back and back into the subconscious, finally to pluck out a festering memory that even the patient was unaware of and that might have since childhood been channeling his or her life into the wrong course.

Pouring out our passions is healthy. We can be sure that in most cases, most of the time, giving free rein to feelings, within limits, helps ourselves, helps those we deal with in the business of daily life and helps our loved ones.

It wasn't always so. A couple of generations back our ancestors would have been appalled at modern shows of emotion. They would tell us to curb our tongues, to remember who we are and to whom we are talking. Feelings didn't rule then; appearances counted. Decent folk kept a check on their innermost thoughts and showed the world only what they thought the world ought to know. A catharsis of emotion revealed an embarrassing affliction; a stiff upper lip was a badge not just of strength but of healthy adjustment.

But now we're lucky to live in an age that equips us with a socially acceptable safety valve to blow off steam. Probably most of us don't vent our spleen enough. I know I don't. Often I know my feelings to be bad and I try to stifle them. It never works.

C. S. Lewis once answered a letter: "Don't bother much about your feelings. When they are humble, loving, brave, give thanks for them; when they are conceited, selfish, cowardly, ask to have them altered. In neither case are they *you*, but only a thing that happens to you. What matters is your intentions and your behaviour."

I have been caught in the same trap as Lewis' correspondent. I have been too hard on my emotions and temptations to sin. I have been ashamed of them. I have tried to make them go away. They won't. I might as well try to put the toothpaste back in the tube. I would be much wiser to try to recognize these feelings for what they are. As Lewis puts it, they are not me but just things that happen to me.

So what can I do? I must stop and take stock of myself. I must sort out my feelings. If they are good, if I feel humility, love courage, I must thank God. If – as all too often – I feel conceit, selfishness, cowardice, the urge to succumb to temptation, I must ask God for help.

At the same time I must try not to bottle up the bad feelings. I must try to let them sweep over me like a wave, swirl right on through me. I must feel whatever is there as fully and honestly as I can.

Now the hard part. I must open the door and let those feelings fly out. I must let them all out, out into the sunshine and the open air. If the world is watching, so be it.

There's a danger, of course. I have to show restraint. I can't just get angry and kick somebody. I can't let disappointment make me a crybaby or impatience injure anybody's feelings. I must make certain that no tantrum ever brings pain to anyone.

But, as far as I can, I have to let myself truly feel. This doesn't mean I have to bare my soul in public or even confide my thoughts to a particular person, although I'm sure that often helps. It does mean that I have to let my feelings run their course. I must not be afraid of them, not try to deny them and shove them back into a dark corner of my mind.

After the tempest of emotions comes the time for calm. Now I can pay heed to what counts. I can remember that feelings are not me but things that happen to me. Now I can examine down into the real core of me, into my intentions and my behavior.

Right here is the moment to turn to God, to pray. After that wind squall of feeling I must ask Him to steady me back on course, to help me make decisions, help me shape my actions. For those feelings may not be me, but what I do with them is indeed me.

So I let the feelings do their thing, feel them to the full, and then let them wash away. Now if I ask God, He will help me know what to do next. He will help me put my emotions aside and He will help me with what counts most. He will show me not only how to feel but, much more important, how to act.

To really believe in God, don't I need to feel good about myself?

I once heard a sermon on the theme that you can only get to know God after you have learned to know yourself. You have to begin by acquiring what we call these days "a good self-image." You literally have to learn to love yourself before you can love God.

I found the idea fascinating because I had always looked at the matter from the other end. To me it had seemed that I must first turn to God, and only then could I truly know myself. Yet I can see the other side of the coin and see why that sermon made sense. The sad fact is that this world of ours is filled with poor souls who have been buffeted by misery into thinking themselves failures. These troubled folk have fallen into such low self-esteem that they actually dislike themselves. From that position it must be desperately hard to reach out to anyone or anything. I can see how, in order to learn how to stretch up to God, they may have had to raise themselves, start to deal with their problems, come to know what they can do and come to like themselves.

But this same world of ours, also sadly enough, is filled with folk like me who tend to have too high an opinion of ourselves. We, too, need a clearer self-image. But we don't need a picture that reveals us to be better than we think we are. We don't need so much to see that we can shine; we need to be reminded that we can be ugly. More than anything, we need a healthy dose of humility. To find God, those of us in this category have to look hard for Him, and we have to take an extra hard look at ourselves.

So, we are all different, and we all have different hang-ups. We have to start with what we have, with the kind of person we are, then work our way to God by the best path we can find. Part of the job is getting to know ourselves. If we do that well enough, we may find that along this path we do indeed meet God.

Isn't it easier to believe if you had a happy childhood?

It would be a fair question to ask of me: Don't your firm beliefs that there is a God and that He is a Father stem from your own childhood? You were happy a child. You had loving parents. You looked up to your father. Hasn't that shaped your faith?

Good question. I did indeed grow up under the blessing of a happy home with loving parents. My feelings today about God could well be related to, and possibly even result directly from, my upbringing, from my earliest memories. My whole notion of a loving God could be all wrapped up and confused with the earthly parents who loved me.

Now suppose the opposite were true: Suppose I had an absentee father or, worse, one who beat and abused me. Would I still today believe in God as a Father? If I had a father who wasn't around or who ruled as a tyrant, might I not today be an atheist or see God as a devil?

Too simple? Of course. But it may be more than pop (forgive the pun) psychology. I do believe that the way I look at God has been conditioned by that loving family life during my formative years. But has this blessing hindered me from seeing God as fully as I might otherwise? Is my concept of Him too close to that of my natural father? Has not the cozy warmth, the sense of safety and comfort that my childhood evokes, colored my picture of God? From the fact that my parents nurtured me do I project a God Who nurtures the universe? Has my upbringing even hidden from me the brutality of nature, concealed the harsh reality of the whole cosmos?

I don't believe it. I believe that my faith that there is a God and that He loves me is based on something stronger than the love my parents gave me. But could I have willed this just because I wanted it to be true?

No again. My faith does not depend on my will. I am more sure of this than ever after considering the views of two German philosophers.

Arthur Schopenhauer (1788-1860) would say yes, I made God up in my mind. Schopenhauer's central thesis is that man is driven always by his wants. What we don't have in life we create. We don't desire a thing because there are good reasons to have it; we find reasons for it because we want it. This mighty force of desire, of self-interest, Schopenhauer calls the Will. Humans, he declares, can go so far as to use this Will to invent their own God.

Is this what I have done?

I would much rather listen to Schopenhauer's near contemporary, Friedrich Schleiermacher (1768-1834). His great idea is that religion is a feeling of absolute dependence on God. Schleiermacher says a person does not find the way to God through reason or through being good. Feelings are what move us to God. Both rationalism and superstition are blind paths. Even spiritual inspiration, even Revelation, even miraculous intervention are beneath the level of real religious experience. They are objective events that can be debated. What counts, Schleiermacher insists, is how we feel. Give free rein to our feelings and we can feel God. We feel we are unconditionally dependent on God and we can be certain that this is good.

For me there's no contest. I side with Schleiermacher over Schopenhauer. My belief in God is based on many things, but surely most of all on my feelings. That's why I trust my faith. That's why I'm so sure.

If I have to keep working at faith, is it really worth it?

I think almost every believer, no matter how convinced, has to face the fact that faith can come and go. On a sunny, happy morning we can feel God to be so close, realize His love so warmly and wonderfully. And then on the next day we can find ourselves inattentive and indifferent and cold.

Is God trying to test us? I don't think so. The fact is that we are not angels or saints. We are human. Faith, like any other emotion or any other process of reasoning, cannot be static. It never stays quite the same. After all, it is filtered through a restless, sometimes preoccupied, sometimes weary and always very human mind.

None of us is immune. Stephen Neill, a noted church historian and eloquent Anglican bishop, once wrote: "Being of radically sceptical temper, I still wake up on about three mornings a week, saying, 'Of course it couldn't possible be true.' But then common sense comes to my rescue, saying, 'Who are you to decide what is and what is not impossible in this wonderful world God has given us?'"

Even John XXIII, surely one of the holiest popes ever, freely admitted to the doubts that come and go. "I have found good reason to blush and feel humble," Angelo Roncalli wrote as a young seminarian. "I have allowed myself to be distracted as soon as I got up. . . . I have made my general self-examination with very little, if any, profit; I have let my thoughts wander. . . . I have given way to . . . languor."

Since these moments of dryness come out of nowhere to plague all of us, perhaps we need not feel too guilty. But faith needs to be worked at. The best way is to pray, to try to regain the wonder of God by talking to Him. This isn't easy; it's hard to keep our minds on the job. One help I've found is a wonderful little Latin phrase, *coram Deo*. It means "in the presence of God" or, better yet, "face-to-face with God."

I use this phrase during my prayers, but I also call it to mind just before I begin, when I am preparing to pray. I focus on *coram Deo*. I remind myself of the obvious but easy-to-overlook fact that in the next few seconds I am going to be offering my thoughts to heaven and I am going to be, in the most real sense possible, actually face-to-face with God. If I am in a dry spell, this can slosh over me like a pail of cold water. It makes me realize that what I am about to do is truly awesome: I am going to have the audacity to tell Almighty God that I am ready to have Him listen to me!

So I pray. And, of course, I should keep on praying, steadily, devoutly, whole-heartedly. And, of course, I don't. Distractions triumph. Those thoughts of mine slip off the rails.

Now *coram Deo* can help once more. I shock myself back to reality. Get with it. I am really, right now, face-to-face with God. That's the jolt I need. I have been daydreaming. God, in His infinite mercy and patience, has been waiting. I pray again, better this time.

But what if the dry period lingers? What if this isn't just a spell of absent-mindedness, of laziness? What if I can't pray because just at this moment I can't bring myself really to believe?

I have an answer, but it could be one that works only for me. When I am really up against it, when I feel heartily sick of the world and of myself, when God seems impossibly far away, when I can no longer in my heart of hearts believe that the Incarnation can actually be true, then I resort to a very private remedy.

I turn to God and I ask Him a question. I make an effort of will to make the question real for me, then I pray that He will answer. And then I put it to Him.

I ask, "Do You love me, Lord?"

In an instant I know His answer. It rushes to me, floods over me. I know beyond all possibility of doubt. He has told me.

God does love me! Me! It's love, real love, and He loves me.

Am I supposed to help myself or "let go and let God"?

Before I became a believer, a question used to bother me: Christian writers and speakers would talk about the ethic of doing good, of trying our best to live the godly life, of working at it as hard as we can. They seemed to believe fully in "God helps those who help themselves." Then in almost the same breath these same wise folk would start talking about how little we really can do, how we should leave everything up to God. All of a sudden their refrains had changed to "Let go and let God."

You can't have it both ways, I used to think. Either the Christian practice is to try hard to do God's will or it is to leave everything to Him. The experienced Christians who spoke almost simultaneously about both concepts didn't seem to see a contradiction. They could quote Jesus to back both ideas.

I just didn't get it. But now that I know the New Testament better, I begin to see how both courses of action might lead to a proper Christian life.

Take that "God helps those who help themselves" theory. Does it mean we are supposed to keep trying harder and harder to be good, aim always at the impossible ideal of loving God with all our hearts and minds and souls? But can this be right? Should we not instead know our limits, realize we can't make it on our own, and so reach a brave decision to surrender and turn our problems over to God?

Now take that "Let go and let God" theory. It's a comforting concept, but can we carry it too far? Isn't there a danger that in our very devotion to God we might be copping out, giving up, leaving all to Him and abandoning our own efforts? Is that what God wants of us? Does He not expect us to use the brains and muscles He has given us?

Surely this is one of the toughest choices a believer has to confront. Moreover, it seems unfair: unbelievers face no such worry. This particular question comes to torment us only after we have discovered God and really want to be good. At this point we know we are loved and we love back. So do we put our love to work by straining every nerve to do what's right? Or do we admit we are powerless and let God take over?

Perhaps the question itself is so impossible, so hopelessly beyond us, that at one level it answers itself. We begin to feel that we really do have to abdicate to God. But if we give up, the wound opens again, we feel the nag of guilt, we despair that we have not tried enough.

What to do?

There is one little word that I know I don't turn to nearly enough: *trust.*

Trust means placing ourselves into God's hands. It means much more than leaving our affairs — our troubles, our fears, our hopes – with Him. It means giving our whole being to Christ. It means handing over all we have to Him, holding nothing back. It means turning ourselves inside out, casting off the old, putting on the new.

As St. Paul taught us, we put ourselves into Christ and we put Christ into us. If we really, freely and fully, give up everything, then there can be no question of a compromise between striving to be good and leaving all to God. We find the answer. We learn that at the very moment we are acting for ourselves, God is right with us, loving us and helping us.

So trust is the key. If we trust enough, we will find ourselves, without even thinking about it, working mightily to do God's will. And at the same time we will find ourselves looking joyfully to God and leaving our very lives and souls entirely up to Him.

How can I possibly give all to God?

All.

That little word has one of the biggest meanings in the language. And it's a frightening word for a Christian trying to commit to God.

To be a Christian is to follow Christ. Jesus never said it would be easy. He made no bones about it. He asked us to give Him nothing less than ourselves. He made it clear He wants all of us, our souls, our minds, our bodies. As Christians, the job of each of us is to pick up our own private crosses, our own private burdens, and follow Him.

When the rich young man asked, "Good Teacher, what must I do to inherit eternal life?" Jesus answered: "You lack one thing; go, sell what you have, and give to the poor, and you will have treasure in heaven; and come, follow me." At that the young man's "countenance fell, and he went away sorrowful; for he had great possessions" (Mark 10:17-22).

Jesus was even more exacting when He was asked, "Which commandment is the first of all?" He did not mince words. His order was only too clear: "You shall love the Lord your God with all your heart, and with all your soul, and with all your mind, and with all your strength" (Mark: 12:28-30).

All, all, all, and again all!

How can a Christian, any Christian, possibly obey such a commandment?

For myself, I must answer yes, I do want to give myself to God. I really do. But how can I give Him all? I want to make a total commitment. I want to say, "Here, Lord, I am Yours. Take me." I don't want to hold anything back. At least I don't think I do. That's the rub. Giving all to God means *all*. I tremble at the very thought. It means that no nook and cranny of my soul will ever be private. It means that, like the Apostles, I must drop everything and journey where Jesus leads.

But how? How, with my settled life, my family, my responsibilities for others, can I possibly do this? What does God expect of me?

I've wrestled with this problem for a long time, and one point I cleared up early on. I'm certain that making a total commitment to God does not mean I have to rush off to join a monastery or take a begging bowl into the streets. God surely doesn't want me to abandon my obligations to my loved ones. In fact, there is no power of heaven or earth that would make me leave my beloved wife or cut my ties to my children and grandchildren. That is so beyond question that I know God would never demand it.

I've come to believe that giving myself – all of me – to God means something different. I don't think God wants me to change my life style much at all. He simply wants me to lead a better life and do a better job at the things I do now. He wants me to be a better husband, a better father and worker and citizen. He wants me to try to get rid of my sins and to love Him while I do all the homey little things I do now.

My life would go on much the same. People would hardly notice. I might seem kinder or more attentive or to have more time and be willing to listen. I might seem to be in better tune with others and, especially, to get on better with myself. Yet I would still be the same old me, muddling on through life, getting up in the morning and getting the same jobs done as best I can. Nothing much would change on the outside.

But if I truly gave myself – all of me – to God, what a difference there would be on the inside! There God, not I, would rule. God would remake me. I would be re-born. I might look the same, but I would know and God would know. I would be new right down into the depths of me. I would be new through and through.

A beautiful dream. How can I achieve it?

Giving away all of myself may be the most difficult task I've ever tried. I need help. I can only get on my knees and ask God.

Isn't it wrong to praise God just so we can live forever?

It seems unpleasantly like a bribe. A worshiper prays to God hoping that by doing so he or she will earn a place in heaven. Never mind faith, never mind love for God; just pray enough, just go to church enough, and you will win the right to everlasting life. Existence here below is, as Thomas Hobbes has said, "short and brutish," right? So this is a real bargain, a cheap, sure way to get to paradise. Bend your knee before the altar and do all that other pious stuff, and you've got it made — forever.

Well, that's not Christianity. You can't buy God, and you can't buy your way into heaven. In fact, I think that for those of us who are beginning to learn about the faith or are struggling whether or not to embrace it, the wisest and safest course is to put all thoughts of the hereafter out of our minds. Why?

If we start to build our faith thinking about the gains it has to offer, we are going to start building on very shaky ground indeed. We are going to find that making heaven the goal is not only an immoral way to true faith but also a counter-productive one. If we are lured to God only by the prospect of reward, we're making nothing more than a business deal: You scratch my back and I'll scratch yours. Believe in God and He'll let me into heaven.

Trouble begins right away. If we have our eye only on that ultimate prize of heaven, our faith can't be real. We start believing for a phony reason, and it gets phonier as time goes on. As soon as life gets rough, as soon as misfortune comes our way, we blame God. Haven't we done all the right things to earn a comfortable life now and ultimately deserve heaven? Then how come God is being mean to us? We find that this phony faith, phony right from the start, is no comfort at all. It was constructed on a wobbly foundation, and at the first setback it topples like a house of cards.

But if we start building on proper ground, if we start believing from the other end, then our faith holds firm. If we begin our faith not because we expect a payoff but because we think God is real and that He loves us, then we are off to a good start. Now we can go on to firmer and firmer beliefs. We can believe because we want to love God in return. We can believe because we want to love Him so much that now we truly love our fellow humans. When we reach this point, we discover we have shoved any thoughts about ultimate rewards to the back of our minds. What we're thinking about most is God and love and how vital and wonderful this life of ours right here, right now, can be.

That is faith built on solid ground. That is the true reward of Christianity.

How can Christians be so sure of the hereafter?

Christians can take comfort in a glorious promise: There is indeed life after death. Jesus gave this pledge to us in perhaps the most comforting words He ever uttered. He made the statement to Martha just before He raised her brother and His good friend, Lazarus, from the dead: "I am the resurrection and the life; he who believes in me, though he die, yet shall he live, and whoever lives and believes in me shall never die" (John 11:25-6).

There you have it. A prescription for eternity. Jesus says it flat out. No equivocating. No ambiguity. He tells us that if we believe, we will know life after death. What we have here now is not the end, only the beginning.

Of course, Jesus didn't tell us much about what this life after death will be like. That raises the whole mystery of Revelation — what God revealed through Jesus and what He didn't. Jesus could have laid everything out, given us a real outline of what we can expect in the hereafter. Instead He gives us only a glimpse. A glimpse and a promise. He must have had a reason for holding back the details. Perhaps He knew our poor minds to be too small to absorb the full glory of heaven. But that can't be the only reason. After all, God could have made our minds any size He wanted.

I think Jesus withheld the facts of life after death for the same reason that He gave us only a partial revelation of Himself. He wants us to use our own minds and hearts to work our way to Him not through certain knowledge but through faith. He wants us to get to heaven not through self-interest but through love.

Of one fact we can be sure. Go back to Jesus' statement: "He who believes in me, though he die, yet shall he live." The word that counts is *believes*. Each of us has to do our own part. We have to believe in God and Jesus. Always we have to be sure to believe in God for His sake, not because we expect rewards. We have to put perfect trust in the Incarnation. We have to believe God really did reach out to us through the life and death and resurrection of Jesus. We have to believe that Jesus lives with us still.

There truly is a gate to heaven. The path to the gate is faith. We have to work at it, but we can find the way. God is waiting.

What right have we even to guess about heaven?

Jesus didn't give us the specifics about heaven. He didn't mean to. But being human, we can't help wondering. After all, heaven is important to us. We may live there forever.

Think of heaven and we see clouds drift across a sea of serenity. We think of halos and harps and angels. We watch faithful St. Peter guarding heaven's gate. Some minds see a darker eternity. They imagine halfway houses like limbo and purgatory. Darker still, they conjure up hell and fires and separation and eternal damnation.

Well, maybe heaven and hell and everything in between will be like that and maybe they won't. We just don't know. What we can be sure of is that, sooner or later, we will all have a chance to find out.

Malcolm Muggeridge came to Christianity late in life and became an eloquent apologist. He put down these thoughts about his own death: "I believe with a passionate, unshakeable conviction that in all circumstances and at all times life is a blessed gift; that the spirit which animates it is one of love, not hate or indifference, of light, not darkness," that it "has been benevolently, not malevolently, conceived." If death, he went on, "is nothing, then for nothing I offer thanks; if another mode of existence, with this worn-out husk of a body left behind, like a butterfly extricating itself from chrysalis, and this floundering, muddled mind, now at best seeing through a glass darkly, given a longer range and a new precision, then for that likewise I offer thanks" (*Jesus Rediscovered*, Doubleday, 1969).

Malcolm Muggeridge's way has to be a truly Christian way: Give thanks to God if death turns out to be nothing. Then thank Him all the more if death really does lead on to new life.

We have a promise from Jesus that the faithful will indeed inherit everlasting life. But I think there is also a good reason in logic why we can believe this to be true. God is infinite, so His love for us must be infinite. Being infinite, this love surely is able to transcend the barrier between human life and human death. Thus, God's love knows no bounds and goes on forever.

Given God's love, can we then make a guess at what heaven could be like?

There is a story of a little girl, the youngest of six children. One night her father felt she might have been a bit neglected during that particular day of family hurly-burly, so he lingered at her bedside after the usual story and tucking-in. He held her in an extra long and loving hug. She clung to him for precious minutes, then reluctantly let go.

"Daddy," she murmured, looking up at her father, "is this what heaven will be like?"

I think that little girl — more perfectly than any philosopher or theologian or saint I have ever read — has captured the essence of heaven. I think that is what heaven will be like. I think we, too, will be nourished by the love of a Father. I think God will do for us exactly what that earthly father did for that little girl. God will love us and comfort us and hold us in His arms.

I think God's love will be the centerpiece of heaven. When we get there we will find that nothing else really matters. Embraced in God's love, we will find ourselves happy beyond our most sublime imagining. God's love, in fact, will shower so directly and so personally on each one of us that we will know nothing less than perfect joy.

What If the whole Jesus story is proved to be a fake?

Debunkers have long harbored the hope that one day Christianity will be proven beyond doubt to be untrue. This could happen, they believe, in all sorts of ways. Bones could be discovered within a tomb, and some super-scientific process could show them to be Christ's, thus ensuring that the Resurrection never occurred. Or some long hidden documents could be found preserved in a cave like the Dead Sea Scrolls to expose to the world that the miracles of Jesus of Nazareth were nothing but clever frauds.

Two millennia is a long time to test the truth of a story, and it's unlikely that even the most imaginative future technology is going to discover much that we don't know now. Still, suppose it happens. Suppose we awake tomorrow to headlines and TV bulletins bombarding us with a new archeological find or manuscript confession or psychological theory that seems to knock the bottom out of Christianity.

What would we do? If the evidence were convincing enough, belief in the divinity of Jesus would be put to a formidable test. Some of the faithful would be devastated. In a worst-case scenario, churches and organized religion might crumble. But it would take far more than this to kill Christianity. I think there are at least three vital facts to consider.

First, we would be presumptuous indeed to think that human failure, even on such a massive scale, could touch the primacy or the efficacy of God. After all, God is used to rejection. We all reject Him at one time or another. I reject God every time I sin, and, heaven knows, I sin often enough. No matter what my guilt, God loves me. Even if we all rebuff Him now, hand Him the greatest rejection of all by denying His Son, He would continue to make Himself known to us. He would love us still.

Second, even if, in some cataclysmic aberration of tradition and reason, faith in Christ was momentarily swept away, the central ethic of Christianity would stand like a bulwark. For twenty centuries we Christians have believed in Jesus and in what He told us about the Father and the Holy Spirit. That has been the most important message. But along with this essential lesson, we have come to believe in something else. This is the morality of Christianity, the teaching Christ left us to live by as Christians. He has been our example. Side by side with our faith in Jesus we have lived with the knowledge of how He wants us to act. So thoroughly have we absorbed these Christian virtues that they have seeped into our minds and hearts. They have settled solidly into the very core of our being. I think this insight, stored deep within us, has become almost indestructible. Even the temporary madness of a loss of belief in Christ Himself would never drive us back to barbarism. The legacy of Christian morality would endure.

The third fact is the simple but crucial one that the reality of Christ can never be disproved. As defenders of the faith, we can summon a vast array of witnesses to demonstrate the absolute validity of Christianity. These witnesses are no less than the legions of the faithful going back two thousand years. Their testimony is that not only have they *believed* the truth of Jesus Christ, but they also have *known* this to be true. They have prayed and their prayers have been answered. They have looked to God and to Jesus for comfort and help, and they have found it. It is their witness – repeated over and over hundreds of thousands of times – that provides the overwhelming evidence that Christianity is real.

So we know the facts of that far-off time when Jesus walked the earth. And we know, too, another fact, every bit as certain. This fact is that it is Jesus Who for all that time has lived within so many of us. We need never fear a challenge to the facts. We need only beware that we keep our knowledge of them firm.

I want to believe, but can I ever be sure?

So, finally, how can a Christian be sure? In fact, can anybody ever really be certain that all this God stuff is true?

As we said at the beginning, there are many paths to faith. The road each of us can take depends on all sorts of things, our family tradition, our upbringing, our education, the fate life holds in store for us, the voices we listen to, what we read and see and cultivate within our minds and hearts.

In the end, I can't even presume to begin to tell you what to believe or how to believe. At the last, the best I can do is try to tell you what I believe and why I believe. And even here, I can only guess at all the factors that have joined to create my faith.

I think I must have started my journey toward faith because within me I felt that blank space that only God can fill. I suspect that this void lies within everybody. I know for sure that it was in me. I wanted to fill it. I wanted to find God.

I think, early on, when I looked about me, I saw evidence that there must be a God. I saw it in the conventional places, the beauty of nature, the intricacies of existence and of all creation that only a divine being could have fashioned. But I'm not sure those were as important for me as other hints. I think I looked most of all at my loved ones. I think my love for them is what, in the most decisive way, led me to God. I think that some-

238

how I projected the love I felt for these very real dear mortal beings into a belief that there must be an overpowering love above everything that makes the universe go.

An odd way to find God? Maybe, but that was my way, and it is the way that has sustained me for a good long time now. I can't shake the feeling that love, really and truly, lies behind it all.

So we come back to the question: How can a Christian be sure? And again, I can only tell you why I am sure.

That love I felt and feel for my loved ones, my wife, my children, my grandchildren, my brother, my dog, the love I truly and joyfully feel for life itself, has translated itself into love for God. I love Him and I feel His love. It is real. Nothing, in fact, could ever be quite as real as this.

That's why I believe the final answer must come from within each of us. I know that for me it does indeed come from within. For me it is the ultimate proof, the only proof that, when all is said and done, really counts. It is called experience. I have felt God through Jesus, and so I know. The knowing and the love are by now an integral part of me, through and through. The strands of that knowledge and that love are intertwined. They cannot be separated, cannot be broken, cannot be denied. Together they give me a gift beyond price, my faith.

For me, it is really just that simple. I pray that it might be that way for you, too.